WHY WERE WE THERE?

WHY WERE WE THERE?

VIETNAM 1966

Jack Morgan

TATE PUBLISHING
AND ENTERPRISES, LLC

Why Were We There?
Copyright © 2014 by Jack Morgan. All rights reserved.

No part of this publication may be reproduced, stored in a retrieval system or transmitted in any way by any means, electronic, mechanical, photocopy, recording or otherwise without the prior permission of the author except as provided by USA copyright law.

The opinions expressed by the author are not necessarily those of Tate Publishing, LLC.

Published by Tate Publishing & Enterprises, LLC
127 E. Trade Center Terrace | Mustang, Oklahoma 73064 USA
1.888.361.9473 | www.tatepublishing.com

Tate Publishing is committed to excellence in the publishing industry. The company reflects the philosophy established by the founders, based on Psalm 68:11, *"The Lord gave the word and great was the company of those who published it."*

Book design copyright © 2014 by Tate Publishing, LLC. All rights reserved.
Cover design by Gian philipp Rufin
Interior design by Jake Muelle

Published in the United States of America

ISBN: 978-1-63185-321-0
1. Biography & Autobiography / Military
2. Biography & Autobiography / Personal Memoirs
14.03.17

I dedicate this book to my wife, my children, my grandchildren, all my dear friends, and my brothers in arms from G-2/7. I love all of you.

ACKNOWLEDGMENTS

I would like to thank two dear friends, Matthew Smith of Smith, Rolfes, and Skovdal and Rebecca McFarland, for acting as my editors and creative revisionists while writing this book. This book would not have been possible without their writing expertise in helping me put my thoughts down on paper. Matt and Rebecca, thank you so much.

CONTENTS

Foreword. 11
John H. Patterson Cooperative High School
 (1962–1965). 13
Welcome to Boot Camp. 25
Infantry Training Regiment 57
Vietnam 69
Operation Hastings 83
Back at Chu Lai 97
Operation Double Eagle. 109
Thirteen Days at Home 115
Operation Hastings II 127
First Operation at Dong Ha. 133
The Rock Pile. 141
Back to the Rock Pile 145
The Philippines and Japan 163
Arriving Home. 169
The Hospital from Hell 173
Epilogue. 179

FOREWORD

My name is Jack Morgan. I wrote my first book, Special Investigations Unit, recently, and it has just been released in bookstores. I have sold many books before its release and have been asked by many people who have read it to write another book as a follow-up to the stories that I still have in my head after thirty-four years of insurance fraud investigations.

After I wrote my first book, I thought of many other interesting and scary investigations. One was when my own informant was so high on drugs he had a gun to my forehead, thinking I was someone else who had come to kill him. His finger was on the trigger, the gun shaking in his hand, and he was screaming at me. Somehow I talked him into putting the gun down. This was after the insured I was investigating had hired a hit man to kill my informant.

If you want to know more about this story and many more, you will have to wait until my third book comes out. I have also been told by many people, after hearing my stories about Vietnam after having too many rum and Cokes, I needed to write a book about what Vietnam was really like.

I decided to write this book based on what an eighteen-year-old went through at a very terrible time in our country's history. It begins with what it was like in 1965, the year I graduated from high school, and then goes forward with everything that occurred in my life between 1965 and 1966, mainly spotlighting my unit in Vietnam, the Golf Company Second Battalion, Seventh Marines. They are still my brothers-in-arms, at least the ones who survived a very bleak day in my memory due to losing so many of my friends in a very short period.

It has been nearly forty-eight years since I was in Vietnam. I reflect back on the years as a marine and all that I survived. I don't know why God chose for me to live while fifty thousand other troops in Vietnam died. I still do not understand why we were in the war, and never will. It was a war we should have never been in. There have been wars since, Iraq and Afghanistan, but the troops that came home from those wars were honored and cheered. Why were we not cheered for, and why were we looked at as some type of disease when we returned from a war no one has talked about since?

Only those who were in Vietnam can fully appreciate the lack of welcome I refer to. We lived our lives honorably, tried to serve our fellow man, and tried to make a difference in our society, even though our society turned its back on us then and now. I do not understand any of this, but I still have faith in our country. I love this country and would gladly give up my life for it as I was also willing to do so in 1966.

JOHN H. PATTERSON COOPERATIVE HIGH SCHOOL (1962-1965)

I was raised in a very strict Southern Baptist family of six children with a loving but very strict mother and father. My mom was a stay-at-home mother. Whenever we were mischievous, we always dreaded hearing her say, "Wait until your father gets home!" We would have to wait all day for the impending punishment, which we knew would be severe. My father wouldn't even ask what we did; he would just say, "Go to the lilac bush and cut a switch." If it was not big enough, he would again give us his trusty pocketknife and make us go cut another one. Some of those whippings are still embedded into my mind even today, sixty-four years later.

My family's frequent involvement with the Southern Baptist Church left its mark on my life too. We were always at church every Sunday morning and evening, and also on Wednesday nights. Additionally, when the church had a revival, we went to church every night for an entire week. I do not regret any of these church requirements, and it was a requirement because we had no choice but to go or possibly face the ole lilac bush again. To this day, I hate lilac bushes.

The reason I say I do not regret the days in church is the fact that it gave me the basics for my belief I have today. I do not profess to be a perfect person, and my wife can attest to that, but I have tried to live a good life, trust in God to lead me every day, and be a good Christian to all of my fellow human beings, whoever they may be.

I think this is what gained me the respect I had from everyone at my high school. When I first got to high school, I treated everyone the same and would defend others who were being bullied. I could do this because of my size. I should mention I was heavily into bodybuilding at this time. I even had a job at a gym, teaching weight lifting for the owner, a true friend of mine named Bob Liles. He was my inspiration and got me started lifting weights, teaching me everything about weight lifting I know today.

I became very strong for my age. When it came time to elect a class president for the sophomore class, some friends of mine put my name down as a joke, and I actually got elected. At first I did not take the position seriously, but after a few months, I realized it was very important to the other students to have someone represent them to the overbearing school we were forced by our parents to attend.

My father had worked hard, but it was difficult for him to make ends meet working in a factory for $100 a week, trying to feed and clothe six children. It was for that reason my siblings and I ended up at the John H. Patterson Cooperative High School, a school that you started in your sophomore year of high school because they would get you a job. You went to school for two weeks and then worked your job for two weeks, and for that period, you made fairly decent money working the assigned job. The only drawback was you got no summer vacation for three years to make up the time you were working. The job assigned to me was at *Newsweek* magazine. I stocked computers for about fifty women who worked the machines. I loved the job because they all treated me like their son, and there were some really good-looking women there. Being a sixteen-year-old, I was in heaven every day.

After being elected as class president, I started negotiating with the school principal and faculty to make changes that were long overdue at the school. As a result of this, I was again elected in my junior year and senior year as class president. This position forced me to become comfortable with public speaking, which I still do every day now for a living. The position also taught me leadership, which resulted in many promotions later in life while I served in the Marine Corps and when I was an Ohio state trooper, enabling me to become a staff sergeant in the United States Marine Corps and a sergeant after only seven years on the highway patrol.

My other job during high school was working at a gas station, which was owned by the father of a girl I was dating at the time. Yes, I was holding down three jobs and also going to school and working at the same time. I bought a car, paid for my own clothes, dates, and insurance. The job at the gas station got a little awkward when I broke up with the owner's daughter, but I still continued to work there. The job was unbelievable, especially when I knew nothing about cars. The owner would leave me all by myself to do oil changes, tune-ups, and other mechanical functions where I had no idea what I was doing, but somehow, I got through it.

After my breakup with my boss's daughter, I was asked by a friend to go on a blind date. I met the love of my life that night. After forty-six years, we have three children and five grandchildren. We dated for over one year, and things were going really well. I had plans to continue with *Newsweek* magazine because I had been training as a linotype operator setting type, and I had become pretty good at it. The only problem was, during my senior year, they phased out the linotype and went to computer typesetting, which put me out of a job overnight. I was devastated and thought my only option at the time was to try going to college to attempt a career change so I could support Barb, whom I was unbelievably in love with at that time, and still am today. She was and is the hottest woman I have ever met in my life and is beautiful beyond my wildest dreams.

I went to my father and asked him if he would help me go to college. His answer was a clear, sharp "I have not sent the others to college and cannot afford to send you either!" I knew I could not go to college on just the money I was making with no assistance.

My good friend, Howard Kelley, had brought my attention to the news, which I was never interested in. I was just trying to live my life, work three jobs, go out on dates with Barb, and be a seventeen-year-old at this time in my life. I started watching the news and discovered America was in a real dilemma: South

Why Were We There?

Vietnam was being threatened by North Vietnam, which was Communist, and the South was trying to establish a democracy. At first, the media was behind the United States supporting the South Vietnamese people with weapons and political assistance.

This was hard for the American people because not too many years before, we had fought to a stalemate in Korea, and it was still fresh in every one's mind. At this point, I should mention there was a huge division among the guys at my school. Many stated they were totally against the war while others were saying we should join up and stop this attack on democracy once and for all, effectively saving the Vietnamese people. I didn't even know where Vietnam was and really didn't care. This was when I was hit by what I call the John Wayne syndrome. He was the all-American hero of everyone my age. Along with not knowing what I was going to do with my life, this created a conflict within me about what was right to do at that time. Many guys at my high school were answering the call of the recruiters, joining up to go and "fight the war!"

At the same time, things at home were not going well. I felt my parents were trying to control me, and I needed some space before I went crazy. I mentioned earlier that Howard Kelly was a good friend, and he approached me one day about joining the Marine Corps on the buddy program; we could stay together the entire four years and pick what we wanted to do so we could probably stay out of combat. He said the Marine Corps promised this, and at that time, there was talk of a draft to start sending troops to Vietnam for support of the troops that were already there in 1965.

Howard said, "Do we want to go in the army, or be real men and join the marines?"

We went to the recruiter, and he said what Howard had told me was true. We could pick what we wanted to do after boot camp, and we would stay together. The recruiter said if we signed up, we would leave for boot camp two weeks after graduation. He was in dress blues, creating a strong impression on a seventeen-year-old male full of testosterone not to be totally drawn in by this image of a real man!

I spoke with Barb about it, and she was totally against it; I spoke with my parents, and they refused to sign my papers because I was only seventeen. I was caught in a massive turmoil, enduring many sleepless nights. I was torn, knowing half of my school said they would flee to Canada if drafted and the other half felt joining up was the right thing, the American thing, to do just as others had done in World War II and Korea.

My parents were against war; Dad was a deacon in the church and had not served in the military during World War II. Barb was against it and did not want to talk about it. Half the guys at school I had played sports with and was good friends with first tried to talk me out of it. They turned to being upset with me because I was going to go fight a nonjustified war. To tell you the truth, I didn't really know at that time what the Marine Corps was, if it was a just war or not, or where in the hell Vietnam even was.

My brain was spinning, but I knew I could not stay in the situation I was in. I had no hopes of going to college, my jobs were enough to put gas into my car and pay for dates, but other than that, I would be homeless. The restrictions at home were choking me, and I was starting to have my concerns about the teachings of my church. We were taught every week at church that if you were not a Southern Baptist that you would probably go to hell. I remember passing a Methodist Church one Sunday morning as my dad was driving the family home. I was shocked when he turned to all seven of us in the car and said very bluntly, "Why do they even bother?"

I finally started getting serious about what decision I would make with my life. I had been raised to be a flag-waving American. Well, almost. My father said the country would go to the dogs if Kennedy was elected because the pope would run the country, not Kennedy. Kennedy would be the first Catholic president. I disagreed with my dad on this, but as usual, the ole lilac bush kept me from voicing my opinion.

I started reading about Vietnam and the situation it was in. I studied about Ho Chi Minh and discovered that he actually fought for the United States against Japan in World War II, leading a guerilla force to fight the Japanese. After the war, we turned our back on him, and promises that were made were broken. I think his hatred for the United States started then. He had become a devoted Communist and was being supported by Red China.

The French had been trying to maintain control of their claim to Vietnam, or French Indochina, as they called it. After trying to stabilize the country, they suffered a huge defeat at Dien Bien Phu, with an end result of the country's division just north of Dong Ha. The North set up their government under communism while the South attempted to set up a democracy.

I remember seeing the president of South Vietnam on TV, and right away, I didn't like this guy because he was surely a crook. President Kennedy was willing to send advisors to South Vietnam in the early sixties, and the American people didn't think anything about it because we were not in a war; they called it a "police action" at the time. We were just supporting the South Vietnamese in establishing a democracy. At that time, the Cuban missile crisis had just ended, and we were all terrified that nuclear war could come at any time. I remember watching Premier Khrushchev banging his shoe on a desk at a UN meeting and thinking he was a devil, and we would probably be fighting them soon in a possible world war.

But for the time being, Kennedy was slowly sending in troops. Then it happened, I remember in high school. I was working at *Newsweek* magazine just before I graduated, and the news came that Kennedy had been shot. I watched in shock as President Johnson was on TV, and it seemed to me that he knew before it happened that Kennedy would be shot.

Everyone has their opinion of why President Kennedy was shot, but I have mine. John Kennedy's father, Joe, was in trouble with organized crime. He used the unions to get his son elected. After John got elected, he appointed his brother Bobby as attorney general. Bobby had a plan to tear down organized crime in the United States, and he made it no secret. I think the Mafia, or whoever Joe was in bed with, went to Joe and told him to have John make Bobby back off from his investigations and complete prosecution of these supporters. I think John disagreed with Joe, or maybe he did go to Bobby and ask him to back off. Either way, Bobby didn't ease up, and I feel John Kennedy was assassinated to show Joe and Bobby they meant business. I also think Bobby would have become president if he himself had not also been assassinated.

Why am I even talking about this situation? Well, after John Kennedy was killed, Lyndon Johnson assumed the position of president, having been Kennedy's vice president. The reason I feel Johnson already knew Kennedy was going to be assassinated was because of the expression on his face and the words he had spoken on the airplane the day he was sworn in. He seemed like he expected it to happen, like he was not shocked. He didn't appear to be distressed at all; he seemed totally unemotional as he was sworn in.

When President Johnson appeared on TV months after Kennedy's assassination, he made this statement, and I remember it well: "Mothers of America, I will not send your boys to war!" About six months later, he had committed thousands of troops to Vietnam, and the number escalated every month for the next ten years, until President Nixon finally signed the peace agreement through Henry Kissinger's meetings with the North Vietnamese.

Until then, Ho Chi Minh worked toward a goal of making Vietnam one country under communist control. The South Vietnamese wanted to be a democracy, and they had already started to establish a government of their own. At the time I read about this, I thought long and hard about how we had freedom and they did not. I wondered, is it my responsibility to fight for their freedom?

During this period, before major US involvement, the North was sending killing squads across the border to eliminate elected officials in villages and was doing everything they could to deter the possibility of a democracy being formed. Vietcong were put into villages and threatened with death if they cooperated with the South Vietnamese government.

Every night before I actually joined the marines, we watched on TV as the situation worsened. I decided the marines would be the place for my friend Howard Kelly and me to make sure we put an end to communism once and for all. But boy, was I in for a shock when I discovered later what was really going on during the time: how corrupt the government was in South Vietnam, how our own government lied to us about our involvement, and the limited war we were fighting for no reason at all.

Howard and I joined up with several other guys from the Dayton, Ohio, area. The recruiter came to our house, and I remember my mother and father telling the recruiter they would not sign the paperwork because I was seventeen and could not join without their signature. I was totally committed at that point and told my parents if they didn't sign, I would just wait until I was eighteen to go anyway. They finally agreed to sign.

I was now a marine.

Later I would realize just how stupid I was by joining, but at the same time, I joined one of the finest brotherhoods of any fighting organization in the world, and to this day, I am proud to say I am a former marine.

The next few weeks after I graduated were uneventful. Barb and I continued to date while Howard and I talked about how many North Vietnamese we would kill. About two weeks after graduation, we went for our physicals in Cincinnati. We were put onto a bus and driven there with about fifty other new recruits to join a group of a thousand or so already there. I remember it was the most humiliating position I had ever been put into in my life. We were lined up in a gymnasium and told to take all our clothes off. I was shocked. They were not fooling around.

Those of us who stood in stunned silence were told to get our clothes off right away. You were given a duffel bag to put your clothes into and put around your neck. There I was herded into a line with the other new recruits as though we were cattle. A duffel bag around my neck, totally nude, as a doctor casually went to each one of us to check our hearts and then to check for a hernia. I had never had this done before, and to tell you the truth, I didn't know what to do or think, so I just stood there, waiting for that part to be over.

After the physicals, we were driven back to Dayton and given our orders to go to boot camp. The DI—drill instructor, that is—asked which boot camp Kelly and I would like to go to.

We asked, "What's the difference?"

He told us we were right on the borderline of being sent to either Parris Island in South Carolina or San Diego in California. We told him we had never been to either state to know what the difference was.

He replied, "San Diego is really hot with lots of blacktop, and Parris Island has lots of sand fleas."

Kelly and I opted to go to San Diego. Little did we know any marine who went through Parris Island would call us Hollywood Marines because, according to them, Parris Island was a tougher place than San Diego. I have never argued with this fact because I don't know if it was true, but I cannot fathom how anything could be worse than what we went through in San Diego in August of 1965.

We got our orders and our plane tickets. I had never been on a plane before. I recall looking out the window, taking picture after picture to show my family when I returned. I was in awe at the sight of the mountains and deserts as we flew over the western states en route to San Diego. It was to be my last glimpse of freedom for a very long time.

WELCOME TO BOOT CAMP

I recall landing in San Diego and being met by an enormous black marine who I remember as being very squared away. I thought, This is going to be pretty cool, and in a few months, I'll have a uniform like that and be as proud as this corporal appeared to be. We would later find out we had just met our first drill instructor. He was nice to us, spoke in a soft tone almost like we were still in high school, and then asked us to get on the bus after collecting our orders. We realized in just a few minutes that this was all a show for the other passengers that were in the airport. I had no idea I was in for the shock of my life.

I had been in fistfights in school and growing up on the east side of Dayton was no picnic, but what I was about to witness was a huge culture shock to a city boy from Dayton, Ohio. The minute the doors of the bus shut, the DIs started cussing at us with every foul word that I have ever heard. Having been raised Southern Baptist, there were words I didn't even know.

Between the swearing, he shouted "Okay, if you ladies will listen up! Fun and games are over. Welcome to the Marine Corps. All of you now belong to me and my other DIs. You have no rights. You are not your mommy's little boy any longer. You are Marine Corps property."

That statement slapped me in the face. I had no rights any longer? I was now property? I thought this was probably like how the Africans boarding slave ships felt as they were being shipped to America. I now had no rights and became someone else's property. Only two weeks ago I had been a little mommy's boy, as he had just described. Incredibly naive, not street-smart, extremely sheltered all of my life, living and breathing in Dayton, Ohio.

The DI told us, "There are no more bleeding-heart civilians around like those in the airport." We were told we were not allowed to speak; we were to sit at attention, with our hands on our knees, looking straight forward, not looking to either side. He said he didn't even want to see an eye blink.

I remember a black guy sitting in front of me chuckled and looked to the right. I had also thought this was pretty funny and wondered if is this guy was serious. What was his problem? My thoughts of also laughing or moving came to an abrupt end when the DI saw the new recruit in front of me move and chuckle. The DI leaped up from his seat, ran down the bus aisleway, and ordered the recruit to stand. He shouted, "You think this is funny? You think I am talking just to hear myself talk?"

Without saying anything else, the DI slammed his fist into the mouth and nose of the recruit, knocking him out cold! Blood shot everywhere from the nose and mouth of the recruit; blood spattered all over several rows of recruits, including me. The recruit hit the floor. He just lay there bleeding. The DI didn't utter another word, casually walked back to his seat, and started watching all of us again.

My first lesson in life and the Marine Corps had just been learned. When you are told to do something, you do it without asking any questions. Just do what you're told. Worry about any ramifications later. I guarantee you no one else on that bus moved a muscle or an eyeball the rest of the trip. I wanted to look over my shoulder at Howard Kelly and ask him, "What the hell did you get me into?" but I did not chance the movement.

After a very long bus ride, we arrived at the gates of the San Diego, California, recruit training depot. The bus stopped. There were these funny-looking huts that appeared to be made of aluminum. I later learned that they were called Quonset huts. I never understood why. There were rows upon rows of them and hundreds of raw recruits just like me standing in row after row on these funny-looking footprints.

Ask any marine about their first day at boot camp and the yellow footprints, and they will just start laughing. The footprints were painted on the roadway outside of the reception center. They were at a 45-degree angle. That was our first lesson in the correct way to stand at attention, the first of many military stances and movements that would be ground into our brains for the next twelve weeks. Sometimes, just to screw with us, the DI would say in succession, "Right flank, left flank, to the rear march." This would result in all of us just running into each other, costing us about thirty minutes of bare-knuckled push-ups on hot asphalt.

We were instructed to place our feet on the painted footprints and not move and stand at attention. I didn't know what attention was and realized this when the DI came up and dope slapped me across the back of the head. He then showed me and the rest of the recruits how to stand at attention, feet at a 45-degree angle, chin up, shoulders up and straight, chest out, stomach sucked in, and hands along the seams of the trousers.

We stood that way for about an hour with no one talking to us and without being given any instruction. I had to go to the bathroom but was afraid to ask. One guy in front of me raised his hand to speak to the DI because I think he also had to go to the bathroom. The DI ran over to him and struck him in the face. Like the recruit on the bus, he went down unconscious. That DI carried a mean punch. I had been in several fights growing up on the east side of Dayton and had been hit in the face before, but it had it never been enough to knock me out. The DI was one bad dude. I decided I didn't need to go to the bathroom that badly.

Shortly after the guy in front of me hit the ground, we were told to run into the closest building and use the bathroom. We did as we were told, and we relieved ourselves. We never saw the guy on the bus or the guy who raised his hand again.

It was about 11:00 p.m., and we had not eaten since lunch. We were ushered into a Quonset hut, where several single beds were lined up. They had no sheets or blankets on them, and we were instructed to lie down and lay at attention, just as though we were standing up, and not move. We lay there about thirty minutes, and no one moved. All of a sudden, the lights came on, and a DI was striking a trash can with a nightstick and hollering and cussing at us and calling us. I can distinctly remember their favorite" they would call us "dirty, rotten lower-than-plant-life maggot MF—ing pukes."

We were then ushered out of our beds and out of the hut, where we were forced to stand at attention on those footprints in the night air for another hour. Then the DI started yelling at us again. After a while, we went back inside, back into bed and sleeping at attention, not daring to move. This went on all night and into the next morning. Footprints. Bed. Footprints. Bed. By morning, I was so disoriented I didn't know where I was.

Some guys were crying, others just mad, and still others downright pissed off. Some of the guys had urinated on their clothes standing at attention, and others had defecated themselves. We were confused and disoriented, and that was what the Marine Corps wanted. We had been told what items to bring to boot camp, and I had spent my last paycheck buying every item I was told to buy, while being very careful not to deviate from anything. For that time, it was a considerable sum of money to me.

When it was daylight, again they got us out of bed and back into the yellow footprints. We had our small suitcase of personal items we had been told to bring with us. The DI returned and told us all to throw everything we had into the large dumpster that was nearby the footprints. The dumpster was already overflowing with suitcases, duffel bags, etc.

I thought, *No way, I bought all of this stuff, and I am not going to throw it away for anyone.* One other recruit beat me to the statement, and for that infraction, he got hit in the stomach so hard he went down in pain and could not breathe. Whoever made the statement "He who hesitates is lost" did not go to Marine Corps boot camp. I am so glad I hesitated that day; it was one beating I did not have to endure. There were many to come, but it was not my time that day.

The DI told us, "We are so glad you pukes brought all these goodies for us. We sell some of this stuff, give some to the Goodwill, and the rest goes to the Mexicans who will bring back your worthless asses if you ever try and escape from here. They are mean and will bring back any recruit not in civilian clothes. You no longer have any civilian clothes, so you are here to stay, unless you want to be hunted down by twenty Mexicans who will bring you back for some shaving cream and toothpaste."

Right then I realized I was on my own. Howard Kelly could not speak to me, and I could not speak to him. You could not communicate with anyone unless you were spoken to by a DI and asked for a response.

I was tired, frustrated, confused, angry, and disgusted with myself for getting into this situation. I wanted to be home. This was only the first night, and the next twelve weeks only got worse. There was never a time I felt relaxed. There was never any free time just to think and reflect on my situation. They wanted it that way. I still have more to tell you about boot camp and what happened, but the entire theory of boot camp is to totally—and I mean totally—break you down mentally and build you up physically. If you thought you were a tough guy, they singled you out right away and would antagonize you into swinging at a DI. I saw several guys do this when they reached the end of their mental stability, and always that night, six DIs would come get the "tough" guy. We would never see him again after he was carried away screaming. I know this is hard for many of you to believe, and some of the following stories of boot camp are even more unbelievable, but I assure you they are true. Find any marine who went through boot camp in 1965 and ask him if I exaggerated anything I mention in this book.

The next morning, we were told to get off the footprints and to get into a formation. We didn't know what a formation was. The DI physically moved us around until we were in what he called a formation. He then said, "Don't move, you will meet your DIs very shortly." Then he walked away. This guy is the toughest I had ever met, and now we are going to meet our DIs?

We stood there for over two hours, and no one approached us. During that time, we had no restroom breaks, no water, and no food. We didn't know what else to do, except stand there, tired, hot, thirsty, and hungry. Meanwhile, my paycheck that had been spent on toiletries was now being used by Mexicans, who, if I decided to try going AWOL, would probably spray me in the face with my deodorant.

After about two hours, two of the meanest-looking black men I have ever seen approached us. The biggest one was about six feet six and had to weigh about 300 pounds. One of the white guys in our group looked sideways at him, and the DI, Sergeant Black, saw him look. He reached out and, with one hand, put his hand around the recruit's neck and lifted him completely off the ground. The recruit's feet were dangling in the air. The recruit weighed about 160 pounds. I could not believe my eyes. I had been a bodybuilder before joining the corps and had lifted some really heavy weights, but there was no possible way I could have done what Sergeant Black just did with one hand.

At that instant, Sergeant Black threw the recruit onto the ground and started cussing and yelling at him, "You looked at me, boy. Are you queer for me?"

The recruit responded, "No, sir!"

Sergeant Black then said, "Oh, so you don't like me?"

It was followed by the recruit's hasty "Yes, sir, I do."

The DI followed the recruit's comment with "Oh, so you are queer for me?"

The recruit again declared he was not.

This went on for several minutes, with Sergeant Black shouting and spitting while the recruit stood, not knowing what to say to get the DI off his back.

This was something the DIs did constantly; no matter what you said and no matter how you answered a question, there was no correct answer. It was the way they brought you down to nothing: no feelings, no personality, no love, just hatred for them. You forgot about your family, friends, loved ones, and you just focused on surviving the worst twelve weeks of your entire life.

I heard other recruits crying at night, threatening to commit suicide. I do remember one guy that snuck out of the Quonset hut one night. I heard him say he couldn't take it anymore and he was going home. We heard he had been captured and sent to the brig. No one ever saw him again.

We finally met our head DI who was a sergeant and two corporals who didn't have much to say. They merely stood to the side. Our head DI, Sergeant Morgan, approached all of us. He was about my height and was a seasoned marine. He was really ugly, and you could tell he was a heavy drinker by the red lines in his face. He told us we belonged to him now, we had no family other than him; he was our mother, father, and girlfriend. And I remember he always referred to our girlfriends as Susie Scratch-and-Sniff. He told us we had no rights, and we signed away our lives when we joined the crotch, as he called the corps.

He walked between the rows of recruits, demeaning each recruit in some way or another, calling the Mexicans spics, the blacks niggers, the Italians wops, the Asians chinks—and then he came to me. He came to me and asked me what my name was. I answered him.

He stared at me. "Your name is Morgan?"

"Yes, sir," I replied.

Sergeant Morgan responded by pointing to his name tag and telling me, "Your ass is mine, boy!"

I knew at that moment I was in for a nightmare of a time. We were then put into formation and led to the mess hall, where we went through the line and told to take what we want but eat what we take. I was really hungry, so I started to eat. This was a mistake.

Sergeant Morgan came to me and asked, "Were you told to eat yet?"

I said, "No, sir."

He made all of us get up and go outside for PT—physical training—without eating anything. This did not go well for me with the rest of the platoon. I learned to hate mass punishment, and I still do to this day. If one of us messed up, we all suffered the consequences. They said it was to build teamwork, but all it ever did was make you hate the person who screwed up because you were being punished for what he did.

You made friends, but they were very few. The blacks usually kept to themselves. The same applied to the Mexicans, Italians, and so forth. I became closer friends with Howard Kelly and found a new friend in Butch Miller. Butch was an all-state wrestler from Iowa. We hit it off right away. His nickname was Frog, because of his neck. He had an 18.5-inch neck, and he would go around with his chin touched down to his neck, croaking like a frog. There was also Stan Musial, and I kid you not, his uncle was the real Stan Musial of the St. Louis Cardinals. He was a really big kid. I cannot remember where he was from, but he came from money. In the corps, this didn't matter, everyone was the same. He was sort of a wimp in a large body and was always getting into trouble. He didn't have many friends and mostly stayed by himself. I tried to be his friend, talking with him often. He told me about his uncle and bragged frequently about the money his family had. I didn't believe him and thought he was just trying to make himself more important than he was. This all changed when we had our first liberty at infantry training.

He told me that he had someone picking him up, and he had a call girl waiting for him. He asked me if I wanted to spend the weekend with him and a girl of my choice, the cost was on him. I still thought he was exaggerating, and I turned him down, saying I had already made plans for the weekend.

I remember when we finally got liberty. We were walking out the gates, and our mouths almost hit the ground when a limo pulled up and a drop-dead-gorgeous blonde stepped out. She walked right up to Stan and gave him a huge lip-lock, then they got into the limo and drove away. I remember Stan smiling at all of us and waving out the window as he rode off. I also remember when he came back from liberty in the same limo, but with two gorgeous women with him this time. He had a grin from ear to ear. We never looked at Stan the same after that weekend, and he wore that cocky grin from then until we went to Vietnam. I don't know what happened to Stan, but I hope he made it home.

I did have one Mexican friend named Lopez. I still can't remember his first name. We stayed together in the same platoon when we hit Vietnam. Lopi, as we called him, was short and fat and very dark skinned. He was a good friend. I also had a black friend named MacArthur who was a constant screwup. The weekend that Stan went away with the hookers, Kelly and I went home with Lopi and stayed with Lopi's mother and father. MacArthur, whom we called Mac, went to Tijuana, planning on getting laid. He went to a house of ill repute, where they took his uniform and all his money, beat him up, and even took his shoes. He had to hitchhike back to the base, where he arrived in his underwear. He never did that again.

We were issued uniforms and all our gear. I remember the first time I was handed my rifle and held it in my hand, realizing this was for real. We had to memorize the serial number and our Marine Corps serial number. We also later had to memorize our general orders, and they were the following:

1. To take charge of this post and all government property in view.
2. To walk my post in a military manner, keeping always on the alert, and observing everything that takes place within sight or hearing.
3. To report all violations of orders I am instructed to enforce.
4. To repeat all calls from posts more distant from the guardhouse than my own.
5. To quit my post only when properly relieved.
6. To receive, obey, and pass on to the sentry who relieves me, all orders from the Commanding Officer, Officer of the Day, Officers, and Non-Commissioned Officers of the guard only.
7. To talk to no one except in the line of duty.

8. To give the alarm in case of fire or disorder.
9. To call the corporal of the guard in any case not covered by instructions.
10. To salute all officers, and all colors and standards not cased.
11. To be especially watchful at night and, during the time for challenging, to challenge all persons on or near my post, and to allow no one to pass without proper authority.

I still remember those general orders to this day.

We were taught a number of things over the next twelve weeks, including hand-to-hand combat; how to bayonet someone in hand-to-hand combat or on a charge; first aid; how to shoot; how to swim; how to climb ropes to get off a boat and into a ship; how to wear your uniform; how to walk, march, stand at attention; how to drill with a rifle; how to make your bed; how to brush your teeth; how to shave.

I remember Sergeant Morgan telling us how to tuck our shirts in; it was called blousing the shirt. I still do that today. He also taught us to carry our cigarettes in our socks so we had no bulges in our uniform. I still do that today. He taught us if you had a fresh blade in your razor, you could complete a full shave without having to rinse the blade. I still do that today. I had never washed my own clothes before; my mother always did that for us. I was taught how to scrub my clothes with soap and a scrub brush, and then rinse then out and hang them on clothes lines to dry. There was no laundry service in the corps.

Out of twelve weeks of training, that is about all Sergeant Morgan taught me. He was a devil in uniform and treated us so badly we all made a pact that if we ever saw him in Vietnam, he would be dead. I know this is hard to believe one could hate another person so badly, but we all did. We understood it was a DIs job was to train us. But there should have been another way to do it. Sergeant Morgan loved his job too much, and either he despised us and considered us a waste of human skin or he had a terrible home life and took it out on us. I later heard Sergeant Morgan died in Vietnam by friendly fire. Just so you know, I did not do it.

We later heard that the DIs had to go to DI school, where they were treated just as badly as the DIs treated us. Maybe they were just taking out on us what they could not take out on their instructors.

We were taught the history of the Marine Corps and tested on every aspect of it. We were taught how to use every weapon the Marine Corps had, and we were able to dismantle and put back together each one of them. We were taught how to shoot the M14, M16 machine gun, 3.5 rocket launcher, .45-caliber handguns, use the LAW—which was a light antitank weapon—and the M79, a portable grenade launcher that looked like a small shotgun. We were taught how to detonate C4, a highly explosive compound. The interesting thing about C4 is that we carried it in our packs and used it to heat our food on occasion when we ran out of heat tabs. C4 is only highly explosive when used with a blasting cap of some kind. When lit with a match, it just burns. We were taught how to throw grenades, how to carry them, and how to pack a pack so everything fit.

Our day would begin at 5:00 a.m. with a bugle blowing revile and a DI banging a nightstick into a trash can, just like they do in *Full Metal Jacket*. We would then have three minutes to get up, get in uniform, and be standing outside in formation. After that, we would then march to the shower, where we had three spigots for thirty guys. You would shower as quickly as you could soap up and get underneath a spigot to rinse off. You had a bar of soap on a rope around your neck. You would then shave as quickly as you could and get back into uniform, being sure to never ever be late for formation because that would cost you a punch in the gut or a severe slap across the back of your head. This entire ordeal lasted for five minutes, and five minutes only. Every day you would have to stand inspection, your body, your uniform, your bed, your gear, etc., and if the DIs found one whisker you missed, you were in for a solid fist to the stomach, a slap to the head, or a hundred push-ups. Some guys didn't even have whiskers, but they had to shave anyway.

We would then march to the mess hall, where we would be given slop by cooks who were pissed off because they were on mess duty instead of being in Vietnam, and they could care less about the food, the service, or us. You would then have five minutes to eat your food, scrape your mess kit into a trash container, and then rinse the mess plate in water and put it into a rack. I later found out all of the food that was scraped into the trash was sold to local pig farmers to feed their pigs.

From there, you marched back to your hut and were told what you would be doing that day: class, physical training, or rifle classes. Every day had physical training starting at 5:30 a.m., after breakfast. It would consist of push-ups, sit-ups, jumping jacks, squat thrusts, and you did them over and over again. I was probably in the best shape of my life, and I thought that this would really prepare me for going into combat in Vietnam. Boy, was I wrong. The problem was, after boot camp, we left for overseas and just sat around for several weeks before arriving in Vietnam. None of us were in shape like we had been by the time we hit Vietnam.

The first day we were in uniform, we went to the barbers. They sat us down in chairs and started shaving our heads. I remember guys with long hair actually screaming when the barbers took the razor and started from one end to the other. They were bleeding from their heads after they were done being shaved. It was an extremely humiliating experience for all of us.

I remember in the beginning of boot camp, the overweight recruits were forced to endure another humiliation. They were only allowed to eat lettuce and water until they lost a required amount of weight. They were separated from the others and called the fat-boy platoon; they had to wear pink tennis shoes until they lost the required weight. I remember watching them and thinking what they had to endure was unforgivable.

If there was one thing I have always hated about the Marine Corps, it was the way they did this to the overweight recruits. I always thought if you didn't want them in the corps, why did you let them in to start with? Why humiliate them the way that they did? It was terrible to watch. They would make them walk around not in formation, and they had to suck their thumbs like little babies. If you have ever seen *Full Metal Jacket*, you have some idea of how they were treated if you remember the one recruit the DI called Baby Huey.

DIs would find someone they didn't like and continue to harass them in any way possible and make fun of them until they broke. And they all did. I remember one day I had all I could take. All three DIs had been on my case. My main problem was that I had tried to help the underdogs in the unit, especially Lopez.

There was one recruit who was a real jerk and kept picking on Lopez. I really liked Lopez, and we had become close. The problem was I couldn't have a fight with another recruit, or it meant brig time. I took a chance and went to the head DI, Sergeant Morgan, and slammed on his door three times, saying, "Sir, Private Morgan requests permission to enter the duty hut, sir!"

The response was, "Is there someone pecking at my door?"

You would have to go through this several times, beating louder on the bulkhead of the door and shouting louder each time with the request to enter. I finally was granted an audience with the DI, and I knew I shouldn't have even asked to speak to him, because the outcome was usually devastating unless you were summoned. I explained to the DI my problem, and he came unglued. This was one of the biggest mistakes I have ever made in my life. I was cussed at, ridiculed, slapped around, and told to never come back again with such a pathetic problem.

I went back to the Quonset hut with the rest of my platoon to find the jerk was at it again with Lopez. I had to make a decision: do I stay out of it and not violate the rules of fighting with another recruit, or do I take action and handle the situation? I had been a bodybuilder before entering the Marines. I was not on steroids, but I could do multiple reps with 320 pounds on the bench press, deadlift 450 pounds, do curls with 55-pound dumbbells, etc. I was a pretty strong seventeen-year-old.

The more I watched this jerk bully Lopez, the angrier I got. No one else was doing anything. The more I thought about it, the madder I got. I ran across the room, grabbed the bully by the throat, lifted him off the ground, and strangled him. I had lost it for the first time in my life, and if some guys had not pulled me off the bully, I might have killed him. He was turning blue. I literally threw him against a wall, and he cut his face.

I didn't know it at that moment, but the same DI had been at the doorway watching the entire episode. Instead of him yelling, cussing, and hitting me like I expected, he just walked away. The next morning, we woke to revile and were standing in formation, and the DI called me to the front of the platoon. He said, "Morgan is your new platoon leader."

I was shocked and scared at the same time. This meant I was responsible for the entire platoon, ensuring everything was in order, everyone was trained correctly, and their gear was squared away. I was responsible for marching them to and from events, schools, and chow. I believe even though the DI could not publicly approve of what I did to the jerk, he did approve and was glad to see someone put the jerk in his place. We never had any further problems with the jerk, and eventually, he and I became pretty good friends.

I managed to get through the week of being platoon leader without any real problems, and then it was assigned to another recruit. Every week after that, it was changed again.

You always hear marines are trained well in hand-to-hand combat. This was not the case with us. We had some hand-to-hand, but it was mainly killing moves and no real self-defense. At that point in the Vietnam War, the Marine Corps were processing as many troops as possible to send to Vietnam as replacements as quickly as possible, so they were cutting some training. I think they mainly prepared us for Vietnam itself, and they did a pretty good job of that, but trust me, no amount of training could prepare us for what we saw and experienced when we set foot on Vietnam soil.

We were trained in bayonet use, which started with using what they called pugil sticks, a sort of broom handle with pads on each end used to simulate a rifle with a bayonet on the end. We had to face off with another recruit, beginning by just beating each other with it to get the hang of it. We were also taught how to use the butt of a rifle to take an enemy down. Then we were trained in how to parry with a rifle by using thrusts with a bayonet. I always wondered why they were dull when they came from the factory and why we were never taught to, or how to, sharpen them. It was interesting when the DI who did the instruction was on a stand in front of the entire company. He was really trying to impress all of us with his skill, so he was over exaggerating every move, screaming with every thrust. We had bayonets on our rifles in practice and would thrust just like him and yell and scream as he did. We were pretty excited.

This all went well until the DI brought up a recruit out of the company to use as an example. The idea was that the recruit would stand there, and the DI would do his bayonet thrusts to the side of the recruit while the recruit just stood there. The DI got overly excited, and when he did his thrust, he actually stabbed the recruit in the shoulder, spilling blood all over. We were all in shock, the recruit was in shock, the DI was in shock, and then the recruit fell to the ground. The other DIs went to his aid. We never saw the recruit or the bayonet instructor again. The next day, we had a new one.

The last test of the bayonet was the charge. We were trained in charging an enemy and were graded on kills with the pugil stick. We went through a process of elimination until there were only two of us left. The victors would have a face-off for the championship. Everything we did was competition to see who was the best, who could do the most push-ups, sit-ups, pull-ups, squat thrusts, shooting, etc.

My friend Butch and I were the only two left. We had "killed" everyone else in the platoon. This meant Butch and I had to face off against each other. This worried me a little because the recruit Butch took out just before our match was in the hospital, and we never saw him again. Butch had charged at the recruit, caught him in the stomach with the pugil stick, and then leaned back, lifted the recruit off the ground, and threw him over his shoulder, breaking both of the recruit's arms.

Butch and I were both in really good shape, but he was larger than I was. I knew I had my hands full. We charged at each other after having agreed not to hold anything back even though we were friends. Butch and I hit each other at the same time. I caught him in the side of the chest with a glancing blow, and he caught me in the neck with a glancing blow. Neither of us went down. The DIs had a conference and agreed Butch won because his was more of a killing blow. We were just glad it was over.

The day we started rifle instruction was pretty cool. We were taught how to assemble and disassemble the M14, over and over again, even with our eyes closed, and I can still do that today. We were taught the muzzle velocity of the round, how to load the 20-round magazine with regular 7.62 NATO ammo, and also how to load with tracers. I think we loaded every third round with a tracer. For those of you who don't know what a tracer is, it is a round that when fired sends off a reddish light when it goes through the air, and at long distances, you can actually see where the round strikes. This is really useful at long distances or at night. However, it has an adverse effect if the enemy is trying to see where you are because they can see where the round is coming from.

We were taught how to clean our weapons and get them ready for inspection. I will never ever forget the rifle poem we always had to say. We would hold our rifles in one hand, grab our crotches with the other hand, and say, "This is my rifle, this is my gun, this is for shooting, and this is for fun!"

There were many other chants we had to learn and yell out while we were running or marching. Most of them were something along the lines of "I don't know but I've been told [with something really dirty here]! Sound off, sound off, one, two, three, four, sound off!" There were other songs too.

Growing up in a Southern Baptist family, if my dad ever heard us utter a cussword, he would see to it we wouldn't be able to sit down for a week. I never heard one come from his mouth. In the Marine Corps, if you didn't sound off loud and clear, you got your butt kicked. So every day, while either marching or running, we would be forced to recite poems while singing them to the same melody, like this one: "I know a girl who lives on a hill, she don't f———, but her sister will! Sound off, sound off, sound off, one, two, three, four, sound off!" There were songs about all colors, and they were constantly referring to your girlfriend as Susie Rotten Crotch. I will never forget that one.

Every so often, we would be standing in the chow line "asshole to belly button." That is what they would say to us, which meant you had to actually be against the guy in front of you, in what they called tight formation. Sergeant Black would stray over to us and start walking up and down, just waiting on someone to look at him sideways. Our DI, Sergeant Morgan, went along with this and did not interfere with his antics.

Finally one recruit would look at Sergeant Black. It was hard not to sneak a look at him because he was so huge. He would immediately come running up to the recruit and start screaming at him, with spit flying from his mouth all over the recruit. "I saw you looking at me, puke. Are you queer for me?"

Naturally the recruit would answer, "No, sir!"

Then the same cycle that had happened before would occur, Sergeant Black implying the recruit doesn't like him while the recruit stumbles over himself, trying to sort out what to say. The recruit always ended up confused, resulting in a slap to the head, a punch to the stomach, or Sergeant Black's famous "grab the throat and lift off the ground" movement.

Sometimes the recruit, confused, would answer with a yes when asked if he was queer for the DI. If he did, then Sergeant Black would say, "So we have a twinkle toes among us." Then it would start all over again and continue until the recruit was so confused he would have blown his own head off if he were given a gun.

We were really afraid of Sergeant Black for several weeks, and then it became a joke among all of us. The worst we would get was a slap across the head or a blow to the stomach, so we actually started looking forward to him coming over from his own platoon and harassing us. It actually got funny after a while because he was so stupid he did the same thing every time. We even started imitating him in the barracks when we were alone just to pass the time. One recruit would have another recruit standing in front of him at attention, and the recruit would go through the whole scenario, and we would die laughing. It was a diversion from being so scared every minute of every day. For that, I thank you, Sergeant Black.

As I mentioned before, we were taught not only how to use many weapons but also about the assembly and disassembly of several firearms. Before actually going to the rifle range for a full week, we were instructed in the live use of hand grenades, mortars, 3.5 rocket launchers, the LAW—which was a light antitank weapon—the M79 grenade launcher, how to set up claymore mines, the uses of satchel charges, and more. Claymore mines were a half-moon block of high-powered explosives that would be connected to a wire. You could either set it up as a booby trap with a trip wire or attach it to a primer and detonate it from a safe distance away. They were extremely effective in an ambush situation set up in the jungle. The funny thing to me was it actually said on the mine, "This side toward enemy." I know that sounds ridiculous, but trying to remember which way to point the mine and not being sure was not a good thing. To avoid any mistakes, it was written in bold letters on each one which way to point it so you didn't blow yourself up. When tripped, it would blow a charge of shrapnel and powder blast at the enemy. If a whole squad of the enemy was in front of it when it discharged, they would all be dead.

Once we learned to use a rifle, we carried and slept with it every day. We would march and march and march. We would drill on the parade grounds endlessly in the hot sun. If we did anything wrong at all, it was assemble then hit the parade ground and drill close-order drills, manual movements done with the rifle, attention, parade rest, right-shoulder arms, left-shoulder arms, salute, port arms, etc. If we messed up during the drill, we would have to lay our rifles down on the parade deck, which was asphalt and probably 150 degrees in the sun. Then we would have to assume the push-up position with our knuckles on the hot asphalt. It would melt the skin on your knuckles from the intense heat. We would have to do fifty to sixty push-ups at a time but to the count of the DI, which would not be fast. I remember all of us having very ugly blisters on our knuckles until we graduated. I still have scars on my knuckles to this day.

During all of this drilling, I remember one day when one recruit in front of me did not have his rifle perfectly straight at the proper angle. The DI went ballistic, came up behind the recruit, and slammed the rifle into the recruit's head. The M14 has a front sight blade that is extremely sharp and angled, and it stuck into the recruit's head. Blood sprayed everywhere. The DI put pressure on the wound, and medics were called to the parade ground. We never saw the recruit again.

I know I've said "We never saw him again" quite often. But it was true. During the twelve weeks of basic training, I think we lost about fifteen recruits to injuries, DI's beatings, and one I remember who went AWOL (absent without leave), and "we never saw him again"!

We eventually left for the rifle range. We thought this would be a piece-of-cake week because we would just be shooting all week. We were wrong. The full pack of a combat marine weighs about seventy pounds. We were told to pack everything we had into our packs and get fully equipped with helmet, magazines, rifles, and everything, just like we were going into combat. We were put into formation and started a forced march. This is a very fast-paced march with full gear. We went to the beach and headed to the rifle range.

To this day, I cannot tell you where we were at. Like I said earlier, I had only been out of Ohio a couple of times in my life to visit relatives in Kentucky. Now I was in California, on a beach with about ninety pounds of gear on me, and it was very hot. We were told the march would simulate an actual combat situation, and we would be told when to enter the water. If we heard a whistle, it meant an enemy aircraft was approaching, and we had to hit the deck.

We started marching, and the DI yelled, "Into the water!" We marched into the water up to our knees, and then the DI blew the whistle. I thought, *You have got to be kidding me!*

But it was no joke. We hit the deck, totally submerged in the water, with all our brand-new gear, our brand-new rifles, boots, even our Marine Corps underwear. The surf washed over us. Then the DI blew the whistle again, signaling the imaginary plane had left. We got up, and he marched us back onto the sand. With everything soaking wet, the sand collected on our uniforms and our boots, and the sand got inside our boots.

This scenario was repeated several times for about a twenty-mile march from where we started to the rifle range. From the sand to the water, into the water, out of the water, back into the sand. When we finally got to the rifle range, we were exhausted, soaked, full of sand, and every piece of gear we had was nearly ruined. We were assigned to Quonset huts and given something to eat. We were then told we had two hours to be ready for inspection. This meant drying out everything, cleaning our gear and rifle, and standing in formation. To this day, I don't know how we did it, but I guess our fear of the DIs made us do impossible things.

We had it pretty good during that week at the range, other than the DIs sitting on you if you didn't get in the proper stance. They actually were pretty nice to us this week because they were in competition for the shooting award with other platoons. I was in platoon 263, and we did win.

The M14 rifle is the best weapon I have ever fired. It is dependable and extremely accurate. In just one week of training on the range, we were shooting at 100 yards, 200 yards, 300 yards, and 500 yards. You have to imagine this as being pretty unbelievable if you think of five football fields end to end and hitting a circle in the center of a human target that is only a six-inch-wide circle. I shot expertly, and I still have my rifle-range scores to prove it.

One thing about boot camp that was amazing was the classes we had to sit through. I remember one where they made Lee Harvey Oswald to be a hero, along with the person that shot the nurses on the University of

Texas campus in 1966. Both of these individuals were former marines, and they would boast only a marine could have made a shot like that. They made these sick psychopaths into heroes. I never could understand that, and I just sat in the classroom thinking, *These are some truly sick people that are now my family.*

I say family because that was all you had; they always stressed our life was not ours any longer and we belonged to the corps. It was stated many times there are only three things that matter in life and they are, in order, God, country, and the corps. Family was never mentioned, so I guess they thought when you joined, you left your family behind, making the corps your family.

I remember our DI coming into the barracks one day and yelling at us that if he had a choice, he would just take all of us out and shoot us, but the general of the base had requested all of us to be present for a concert in the auditorium. He said that the Everly Brothers, who were former marines, had come to the base to put on a show for the recruits.

The DI said, "I don't have a choice on this, but I will be watching all of you, and if I think anyone is enjoying the show, you all will pay later. You will sit at attention and not move. You will not clap for anything. You will not enjoy the show in any way. Do you understand me?"

We all screamed, "Yes, sir!" and we marched to the auditorium. We sat at attention, and no one moved for an hour and a half. I did like the Everly Brothers, and even though I didn't show it outwardly, it was one of the best one-and-a-half hour of my life because it gave me the time to be totally absorbed in the show and not be where I was, in hell for these twelve weeks of my life. I don't know if either of the Everly Brothers will ever read this, but if they do, I thank you from the bottom of my heart for coming to boot camp that day and giving me some much-needed time to myself.

I guess one of the things that I held against Sergeant Morgan more than anything was the awarding of the dress blues to one recruit. I had worked very hard in boot camp to get this honor. One person out of every platoon was awarded by the DI a full set of dress blues, which were very expensive. It came with a promotion to private first class, a pay grade, and a stripe above *Private*. I was in the running for the award. I had maxed out on all testing, done great in the PT portion of the twelve weeks, and had qualified as an expert with the rifle. I just knew I would get the blues and was proud of all the hard work I had done. The day before it was to be announced who would receive the blues, someone in the platoon screwed up and really pissed off the DI. I remember him saying, "I will show all of you!"

There was one person in the platoon who was what we called a kiss ass. He would suck up to the DIs, and he was their gofer. He was the smallest guy in the platoon, so we called him the house mouse. He would shine their shoes, get their coffee, and do about anything they told him to do. I did not like this little twerp because he thought he was protected and could get away with anything. They announced the six people who made PFC, and my name was yelled out. I stood proud, waiting to hear which one of the six would get the blues. I saw the house mouse had been promoted also, and it made me sick. Then they yelled out his name as the one who got the blues. I was devastated; Sergeant Morgan had given him the blues just to spite the rest of us.

The last day of boot camp was probably one of the proudest days of my life. Before that is my marriage, the birth of my children, their marriages, etc., but that day was special. We got to put on our uniforms for the first time, and we looked good, spit and polish all the way. We went to the parade ground, and the general of the base was there with many parents of the recruits. My parents had not been able to come. We marched in front of the spectators—proud, standing straight, and looking good. We had survived everything that Sergeant Morgan had thrown at us, and we were graduating that day. We would be allowed to have about an hour after the ceremony to pack everything, eat a good meal with cake and ice cream, and then get on the buses to go to the infantry training regiment, or the ITR. We thought it was over and everything after this day would be good.

Sergeant Morgan came by each of us and wanted to shake our hands. I know that many DIs would tell recruits who graduated they had to be tough on them, and many DIs were tough, but their recruits respected them. I did not respect Sergeant Morgan. I hated him, and God forgive me, but I hate him to this day even though he is dead. I refused to shake his hand. I thought I would get pummeled, but there were too many people around for him to do anything. His face became beet red, and I just smiled at him, hoping in my heart I would see him again someday wearing sergeant stripes of my own, and I would beat him to a pulp.

I got on the bus for ITR with the rest of my fellow marines. I saw Sergeant Morgan turn his back on us and walk away to receive his new platoon of recruits, who had no idea of the hell they had signed up for.

INFANTRY TRAINING REGIMENT

When we got to ITR, which was a short drive from San Diego to Camp Pendleton, California, we got off the bus and thought we would be treated as human beings for a change. We were wrong. We were back in boot camp again. The only thing different was that we could go at night to the pogey bait store to buy junk food. Every once in a while, we would get a weekend pass and could go to Los Angeles, Oceanside, or Anaheim. This was really funny and an eye-opening experience. You must remember I was from Dayton, Ohio, and had been to Kentucky once, but that was it. When I saw the big cities, it was overwhelming to me and many of the guys with me.

Most guys thought they were going to get lucky, but their odds were not as good as they hoped. The cities would be invaded by hundreds of horny marines and not many girls. I wasn't even looking because I had Barb at home. I took on the job of trying to keep my friends out of trouble. Drinking was a problem because most of the guys had not been around liquor before. They got staggeringly drunk most of the weekends. The police were just waiting for us to do something stupid so they could take us to jail. They did not like marines.

There were women in these three towns who knew about an insurance policy we all took out before we went to Vietnam. The policy was for $10,000, and you had to name a beneficiary. Later, in 1966 and 1970, there was a big news report that there were women in these towns married to several marines at the same time. They were usually about twenty-five to thirty years old, and they would prey on the seventeen-to-eighteen-year-old marines in the bars. They would marry as many of the marines as they could, hoping they would get killed in Vietnam, allowing them to collect $10,000 for each one they married who died. I read in late 1966 that some of these women collected over $100,000 because so many of us were dying during that time. This occurred in late 1965, before we shipped out for Vietnam.

I will not mention this friend's real name because I don't want to cause any problems in his life, so let's call him Sam. My friend Sam met one of these women in a bar we were at, and he immediately fell in love, even though he had a steady girlfriend back home. I didn't think too much about it at first, but he met her several more times on his leave time. Finally, one day, he approached me to tell me he knew he was in love and he was going to marry this girl he had met. I tried to talk him out of it, telling him she was older and was just using him. He turned on me and said I was just jealous. I got together some of our other friends and told them about what was happening. We had no idea how serious this was and how close Sam came to ruining his life.

Sam turned on all of us and threatened to fight us if we wouldn't go along with him. We protected Sam by not letting him go into town for three weekends. We also told the ITR trainer about the situation and described the girl to him. He contacted the police, and we heard later the girl was arrested, having already collected six times on insurance policies. Sam was devastated but eventually thanked us for saving his life by not letting him be around this woman again. He later told us he had planned on getting married the next time he went to town.

Advanced infantry training was a real challenge. At the end of those four weeks, we went to guerrilla warfare school where they actually taught us about Vietnam. We trained in ITR for three weeks and then guerrilla warfare for another full week before being allowed to go home on leave for two weeks. I remember this was a good time, because I was able to be home for Christmas.

ITR consisted of learning to use all of the weapons available to the infantry at that time. All the weapons we learned about before and some new ones like flamethrowers, mortars and grenades of all types, and Willy Peter. The Willy Peter was the worst form of weapon that has ever been invented, and I hated to even carry it. I was afraid the North Vietnamese would find some discarded or take them from dead marines and turn them on us. It was a white phosphorus grenade that when it exploded would send shrapnel burning with white phosphorus into your body. It had to be the most agonizing death I could think of, other than possibly a flamethrower.

I remember the most fear you had was being in the hand-grenade hole and someone dropping the grenade after pulling the pin. The old term in the corps was that you didn't know whether to "s—— or go blind." I never understood that phrase, but you knew when someone said it they were serious.

This actually happened to me while I was in the hole with the instructor and another recruit. He pulled the pin and dropped the grenade, and then he froze. I didn't know what to do. The instructor let out several volleys of curse words and grabbed the grenade, immediately throwing it over the side of the hole. He pulled us both down into the hole. It exploded almost immediately after he threw it. If you have never been in the service, a normal hand grenade after the pin is pulled has a seven-second delay before it explodes, and when it does, the killing radius is about that of a mortar, between five to ten yards. I was glad that the instructor had it in him to maintain his cool and get rid of it. He acted like this sort of thing happened every day, but I didn't sleep well for several nights. The same guy who dropped the grenade did it a second time. This time, he was taken away, and we didn't see him again.

The food was better at ITR, and they didn't treat us as bad as they did in boot camp, but they were still jerks who regularly went overboard with the discipline and cruelty. The most fun I had at ITR was the nights we would do full maneuvers in full gear. We had blanks in our guns. It was almost like playing soldier when I was a kid, but there was more action, and it seemed more real now. We would be given an assignment to attack a hill or hold a hill. Then we would start over and do maneuvers again. The worst part of maneuvers was the barracks we had to stay at during those nights. After we were done with the maneuvers, we went to the barracks. They were from World War II. There was no heat and no running water. It was about 30 degrees, and we nearly froze to death, even though we slept in our clothing and field jackets.

The scariest thing that happened in all of boot camp, ITR, and guerrilla warfare was going through the range where we had to low crawl under barbed wire all while wearing full gear, while a live machine gun fired, strafing back and forth over our heads. Meanwhile, there were explosions constantly going off just a few feet away from our heads. This was supposed to expose us to what it would be like under real live fire. I cannot testify to this because I did not see it happen, but we were told about a week before we did the live-fire crawl through the barbed wire that one recruit had stood up during the crawl. He had been killed.

In guerilla warfare school, we were trained in how to avoid them and spot booby traps, such as how to spot a punji pit, a hole in the ground about ten feet deep with bamboo stakes waiting to impale you. The pit would be covered over with fake soil and leaves, so when you stepped on the pit, you would fall through to your death on the sharpened bamboo below. It was a terrifying device. We were also trained to watch out for trip lines made of fishing wire strung across a trail where it would either be attached to a grenade or a 60-mm mortar. They called this a Bouncing Betty.

What happened when you tripped the wire was that the pin was pulled on a grenade, and in seven seconds, it exploded, killing anything within five to ten yards.

In addition to Bouncing Betties, there was a trap the North Vietnamese called spider traps. These were holes in the ground dug just deep enough for a man to hide in. The top of the hole would be covered with a sort of lid that could be covered over to look like the normal terrain. A North Vietnamese would dig one of these holes and make a "spider trap" along a trail or area where he knew that the marines would be passing. He would wait until the last several men had passed by and then pop up out of the spider trap and start blazing away right up behind them. It meant almost certain death for anyone caught in his sights, totally unaware that he was there.

We were also told to be careful of the heat, take salt pills regularly, drink plenty of water, and watch for insects. We learned how to use the mosquito repellant, how to dig holes, how to bandage another marine if he got hit, what to do with snakebites, how to use a radio in case everyone else with you got killed, and many other things. You were taught how to make sure your rifle barrel was not jammed full of mud after dropping from a helicopter into a rice paddy. And above all, we were taught how to keep our M14s clean and well-oiled in the hot, humid, and sometimes rain-drenched country we were going to.

After all of the training in ITR, it was strange when all of the training just came to an abrupt end and we were allowed to go home. The training had started in

Why Were We There?

August of 1965, and now it was December and we were free. Well, sort of. We had been in something worse than prison for four months. We had been told when we could talk, when we could sleep, when we could eat. All the while, we were being cussed at, struck, and made to feel like we weren't human beings anymore. Worse than that, they had taken away all our lifelong personalities and molded us into something that our friends, family, and loved ones could not understand anymore. If I heard "You seem different" one more time, I would start screaming.

Yes, we were different. We had been taken from a normal life, put through things that were almost beyond human endurance, both mentally and physically, and our main emphasis for four months was not snuggling with Susie Rotten Crotch. Nor was it going to school and church and just being a teenage guy. We spent four months of our lives eating, sleeping, and drinking how to kill, not just with a rifle or knife but with our bare hands. To this day, I still feel like I could handle any situation that comes my way because of the intense training the Marine Corps gave to me.

I came home for Christmas and again had a great time on leave. I got to have home-cooked meals for the first time in months. I got to see Barb every day, and we had a great time. We even met up with Kelly, Murphy, and some other recruits in the Dayton area. We had a big party at Murphy's house. It is really cool to think that Mick Murphy actually married my favorite cousin, Gloria, later in life. I will never forget Mick and I harmonizing to ole Stewball in his basement; we were the hit of the night.

I know it sounds crazy after all the complaining I have done about the treatment we got in boot camp, but after a few days at home, it was kind of scary. I had been used to a very structured life for months, not really having to think for myself, just doing what I was told. I started to actually miss the structured life and feeling the pride of being a marine. While I was home, I didn't feel proud. The antiwar movement had just started, and I didn't want to be around it. The people back home didn't know what they were talking about. We were going to war to save a country from communist takeover, and didn't they understand that?

The two weeks went very quickly, and before we knew it, we were all on a plane headed back to Camp Pendleton in California. We thought we would get off the plane, go to the base, and head for Vietnam. This was not the case. The first thing I experienced was my first hangover. We got on the plane, Kelly, I, and three other marines we had been to boot camp with. The stewardesses didn't have anything to do because the plane was almost empty. They quickly discovered we were marines headed to Vietnam. They started feeding us free booze. I was a nondrinker, and it didn't take long for me to get totally wiped out.

I do not remember the flight, I do not remember getting off of the plane, and I do not remember anything the entire next day, until I woke up and was told by Kelly to get dressed for mess duty. I put on my uniform and wore it for the next thirty days. We would do mess duty for eight hours and then we would run, do PT, run, and do PT. We were probably in the best shape of our lives. I ballooned from 200 pounds to 230 pounds and lost an inch on my waist. All we did was eat, run, and work out. Later, when we arrived in Vietnam, I discovered why they did this. With the heat reaching 120 degrees every day and not wanting to eat, I lost 50 pounds in thirty days; I was like a human skeleton.

While on mess duty, we had plenty of liberty, so we enjoyed going home with Lopez. He would let us crash at his house. We went to Los Angeles and put our training to use in avoiding arrest by the police on many occasions, especially when we were caught urinating in a neighborhood street and had to outrun the police. I am not so proud of that one. The rest of the stories about what we did and the trouble we avoided will be kept to myself, and in the memories of all the guys who were with me.

After thirty days of mess duty, we were told we were shipping out to Vietnam. We were given brand-new gear but no weapons. We packed and unpacked. We told each other what heroes we were going to be and that we would all come back and be friends for life. I am sorry to say that most of the guys that I left California with that day in January of 1966 did not come back, and of those that did return, I have not spoken with any, except for Kelly. I only saw him once, and he was very standoffish. The only reason I can think of for his behavior is he might have felt ashamed. After we were in Vietnam a month and had been sent to separate units, his father died. Being the only surviving son, his mother applied for him to get out of the Marine Corps, and he got sent home. I have to admit when I heard about this, I was really upset. He was the one who had talked me into joining the corps, and now I was in Vietnam fighting while he went home to his mother? This didn't sit too well with me at the time, but, Kelly, I have changed my mind. You were the lucky one to get out of that hellhole, and I have no animosity toward you at all.

We got aboard planes at El Toro Air Base in California and flew to Hawaii. I thought, *Wow, this is really going to be cool, getting to go to Hawaii.*

I remember looking out the window and seeing the most beautiful island I had ever seen, but when we landed, I found out that is all I would get to see. They had MPs (military police) there as soon as we got off the plane. We were herded into trucks and taken to a barracks, where we were told to bunk down and not leave the building. We couldn't even go outside. I remember it being very warm there. I asked an MP what was going on and why we were being treated like this. He said the higher-ups had decided we should not get liberty because they were afraid we wouldn't come back. I think about that now, and you know what, they were probably right.

The next morning, bright and early, it was back on the trucks. No hula girls, no leas, no pineapple drinks, no alohas, nothing. We were put back onto the same plane and took off saying good-bye to Hawaii, or what little of it we got to see. Most of us agreed, even though we would have probably gotten seasick, we would have rather taken a ship for thirty days. It would have delayed the combat for a while.

I remember we first landed in Guam and then Wake Island before eventually landing in Okinawa. They did let us walk around Guam and Wake Island. If you're wondering why there and not Hawaii, they are both quite small islands with no place to run to. I remember sitting on the beach there by the airstrip, probably eight thousand miles from home, feeling very lonely and forgotten. We did see some pretty cool stuff there leftover from World War II, bunkers and other visible remnants.

We left Wake Island and landed in Okinawa. I think we were there for a few days, but I really don't remember. I know we were not allowed to leave the base, and there wasn't much to do. I remember there were about twenty of us who were pretty religious, in many different faiths. We discussed religion often when there was nothing else to do. On the night they announced we were headed to Vietnam the next morning, they said there would be church services for all faiths starting at 6:00 p.m. going until midnight. The twenty of us who were religious got together and decided we would not go to one or two of the services, but we would go to all of them, just to make sure.

I had been raised in a neighborhood that was predominately Catholic, and other families had no church affiliation whatsoever but were good people. My dad would try to get the entire neighborhood to come to church with us, though few ever did. Dad tried to live a good Christian life, and he was respected for this in the neighborhood, but I really think he secretly thought they were all going to go to hell if they were not baptized in the Southern Baptist Church. I think some Southern Baptists are going to be shocked when they get to heaven and there are people there from other denominations.

That night, the Baptists and Jews went to the Protestant service, the Methodist and Church of Christ went to the Jewish service, and so forth. I think we ended up going to five services that night. I thought it was really funny when our Catholic friends went to all of the services also, even though they were not allowed to by their church at that time. We took Communion at all services that offered it. Even though we were not allowed to at the Catholic Church, we did it anyway.

The one thing that I remember about that night is this: I had twenty friends whom I had been with for four months. We were like brothers. We all came from different backgrounds, different states, and different religions, but we had one thing in common. We cared enough about each other to be there for each other and not let one or two guys go to a church service by themselves. We all went together as one body in Christ—well, except for the Jewish guys. I hope it meant to them what it meant to me. We were about to become soldiers, fighting in the jungles, maybe even being killed or wounded, but this night was special, and I will never forget it. I can remember all of us sitting in two pews at one of the services. There wasn't a dry eye in those rows. We were all holding hands and praying, each one in their own way, praying for ourselves and each other.

VIETNAM

I remember getting up the next morning and all of us being separated. Some of us stayed together, but not many. I remember Lopez coming with me, and that was it. The marines needed replacements badly all over the combat zone from Da Nang north to the demilitarized zone.

Lopez and I were sent to Chu Lai. I think we arrived at the Chu Lai airstrip by plane, but we might have landed in Da Nang first and then ridden in a chopper to Chu Lai. I don't remember, and it really doesn't matter. I do remember the smell as soon as I got there. It was a dirty, fishy, hot, damp, bloody smell that made you want to vomit as soon as you arrived. It was not like I thought it would be; we arrived at an airstrip where mostly F15s and Phantoms were taking off, along with C-130 cargo planes. It was a scary place. I remember not knowing what to expect. Would I get shot as soon as I got off the plane?

We stood there with our orders in our hands, not knowing what to do, with everyone walking around shirts off, trousers unbloused, and not many of them carrying weapons. I later discovered this was a side of the Marine Corps that we didn't even know existed:

the air wing. They were mechanics, crew chiefs, pilots, cooks, and supply men. And they were everywhere.

I later discovered the battalion I was going with was used to guard the outer perimeter of the air base against attack. They were pretty secure there. We stood out like sore thumbs; everyone knew we were fresh replacements, and no one gave us the time of day. We asked what we should do and were told to just wait until someone came to pick us up. About an hour later, a jeep pulled up. "Are you Morgan and Lopez?"

We said yes, garnering the response of "Get in and welcome to Vietnam." He was a pretty nice guy, the captain's jeep driver. He drove us about an hour on winding roads going up and down hills until we finally arrived at the company command post situated just outside of a small village. There we saw our first Vietnamese. The women were beautiful, I thought, they were dressed in either black pajamas or black pajama bottoms with a type of a dress that went down past their knees. They wore funny-looking round hats. Most of the men wore shirts and trousers. They all wore sandals made out of rubber from tire treads. They all were smoking, even the little kids who usually wore a shirt and shorts. I was shocked to see marines giving them cigarettes. They were little kids who couldn't have been much older than eight or nine years old. I later found out if you didn't give them cigarettes, they weren't friendly to you at all. I was also shocked when these beautiful girls and women opened their mouths to reveal blackened teeth. This was a result from chewing a drug called betel nut. It made their teeth and gums unappealingly black.

The captain's jeep driver drove us through the village, but we never saw where the people slept. The village was just a place for the villagers to sell their wares to the marines and bum food and cigarettes off them. There were girls who would do your laundry, and there was a barber. I later learned all the guys just called him Papa Son. He was really short and had about ten kids. He was a nice guy during the day, but I always wondered if he was a spy for the Vietcong, reporting to them every night about what he heard during the day cutting our hair.

None of the villagers could speak English except for some broken words, which was a huge problem because the marines were not trained in Vietnamese before we got there. We had to make do with whatever we could pick up. We were able to catch the words for *good*, *very bad*, *crazy*, *sorry*, and many others, including *dee dee mow* (which was "Get away from me right now") and *no com bech* (meaning "I don't understand"). I know there were many other terms we used that both sides understood, but I cannot remember them now.

I remember meeting the captain. He welcomed us to the company, which was the Golf Company Second Battalion, Seventh Marines. He informed me I was going to be assigned to second platoon, second squad under Sergeant Wenger. The captain said normally we would have had a lieutenant, but he had just been killed, and they had not sent a replacement for him yet. Sergeant Wenger was a gunnery sergeant and was called the platoon sergeant. I was also told my squad leader would be Sergeant Lonnie Saxon, whom we were warned to never cross because he was one mean son of a b——.

For those of you who are totally confused at this point, a squad is made up of four fire teams, with four men in each team. Each team has one man who always has his rifle on fully automatic; the other three have theirs on semiautomatic to save ammo during a firefight. You do have the option of switching to full automatic if the s—— hits the fan. One senior man in the fire team is called a fire team leader. In the platoon, you have four squads, each squad being led usually by a sergeant. With each platoon, there is a commander, who is usually a second or first lieutenant. Then with each company, you have four platoons, with the company commander being a captain. The platoon commander has a platoon sergeant, who assists the platoon commander, and the captain has many staff in the company headquarters assigned to him for various tasks.

With each company, you have machine gun squads and teams, mortar teams, 3.5 rocket launcher teams and flamethrower teams. In each battalion, there are four companies, led by a battalion commander, usually a major or one of higher rank. In each division, you have four battalions, and each division and battalion has many support staff and members for various functions. Scouts, intelligence, supply, mess and cooks, chaplain, and to each platoon is assigned one to two navy corpsman.

We were told to walk to a certain area closer to the front lines past the village. There we would find Sergeant Wenger waiting for us. We went to his tent. He was probably one of the meanest guys I have ever met. I would later learn he cared more about us than any of the other sergeants I had ever met before. He smoked and drank more than anybody. He had an assistant platoon commander who was a senior sergeant, but I cannot remember his name. He told us where to go to meet our squad leader and left us two words of parting advice:

1. Never, ever go to sleep on guard duty.
2. When the s—— hits the fan in the bush, do what you were told, and you may make it back alive.

That was it—no long speeches and no threats of any kind. Lopez and I thought this was going to be a pretty good assignment. We walked farther past Sergeant Wenger's tent and came to a smaller tent, where we met Sgt. Lonny Saxon. Lonnie was tall and as mean as a snake. He was from North Carolina. I will never forget what he told us the first time we met him:

1. Do what you are told.
2. Never fall behind, or we will leave you.
3. Keep your rifle and equipment clean.
4. Watch out for each other; we are all we have over here, and if we don't watch out for each other, we are dead.

5. If anyone in the squad gets a package from home, it is shared by everyone in the squad; we are family.

6. If you ever get caught by me asleep on guard duty, I will give you a choice: I will write you up and have you court marshaled, or I will beat the holy s—— out of you, and no one will ever know.

We believed him, and I don't remember Lopez or I ever going to sleep on watch. This was very hard not to do because everyone had to stay awake until midnight, then you would switch off with your foxhole partner every one and a half hours. It went in shifts of watching for one and a half hours then sleeping for one and a half hours until 6:00 a.m., and then everyone along the line would be awake watching for an early-morning daybreak attack. It was hard not to fall asleep when we had been up all day working doing various things: filling sandbags, making water runs, helping at the chow hall, cleaning gear, doing PT, and whatever else needed done around camp.

Our lines were on the outer perimeter of the airstrip, as I stated earlier. We had bunkers with a field of fire that, when activated, would make a killing zone with fully automatic weapons hitting every foot of the zone in front of you. The bunkers were spaced just right so the fire would meet the bunker's fire on the left and the right when you traversed your fire.

When the South Vietnamese were not working in the rice paddies in front of us during the day, we would have practice fire on a simulated attack of our positions. I think I remember every third round that came out of the magazine was a tracer round. A tracer round was a round that, even in the daytime, you could track the trajectory of by seeing the white phosphorus glow it gave off from when it left the rifle until it struck its target.

We used to have practice firing in the killing zones as if under attack. This turned out to be fun because Sergeant Saxon would let us take a few potshots at Hill 285, where we knew the North Vietnamese were watching us every day, checking for any weak areas they may be able to attack. We took several potshots at Hill 285 just to make them aware we knew they were there.

The M14 has an effective range of over five thousand yards, and Hill 285 was about three-quarters of a mile away from our bunkers. It was an easy target. We could also check out our weapons in case we needed to shoot at that range for real. With the tracers, you could see exactly where your rounds hit, and you knew right away if your sights were aligned properly. I always wondered if I killed any North Vietnamese with these practice firings.

My foxhole buddy, Mike Allen, and I became close friends. Mike took me under his wing and started teaching me everything he could: how to watch out for booby traps, how to keep your rifle dry in the rain, etc. The movies show marines putting rubbers over the ends of their barrels, but we were just sure to never have the barrel elevated, always keeping it pointed down. He taught me how to make a jungle sling out of my rifle sling; you would take it to its full length, and put the sling over your shoulder, resulting in the weapon being suspended about waist high. This way, if you were on a trail and things got out of hand, your rifle was at the ready, and you could just start firing from the hip. This was also important if you had the weapon on fully automatic because the M14 had a tendency to rise when fired on full auto. You could put your hand over the flash suppressor and push down so the rounds went fairly straight instead of half of them going up into the air.

Mike was one of the few guys I first met there who would actually give me the time of day. I was a boot, and most of the other guys with G-2/7 had been there for eight months. They were some of the meanest guys I had ever met. They were dirty, and they smoked and drank all the time, at least when they could get their hands on alcohol. They were ruthless when it came to the enemy. They had been in many operations and killed many Vietcong and North Vietnamese, including civilians. I think most of the civilians killed were by accident, but I am not sure. These guys had the so-called thousand-yard stare of being in combat, and they didn't care if they lived or died. The one thing that I want to mention is that the training Mike gave me was invaluable. It saved my life many times. Later, when the rest of Mike's group rotated back to the States, I became the ole salt, and the new guys looked to me for training in how to stay alive.

When I first got to Vietnam, it was excruciatingly hot. I had come from Ohio weather in the teens when I was on leave, and then when I arrived in California before we went to Vietnam, it was in the 60s. When I hit Vietnam, it was 120. The first few days there, you sweat profusely and you cannot eat. While at the base camp, you could get a shower and put on some clean clothes, but by the time you got halfway back to the bunkers, those clean clothes would be soaked through from the heat. You are not hungry at all because of the heat. Mike kept trying to get me to eat and drink all the water I could, but I still got sicker than a dog for about two weeks. I think I lost 20 pounds in a week. In the next few months, I dropped from 220 to 150.

When we were at the base camp guarding the airstrip, we would take turns making the two-mile trek from the front line to the mess hall to eat. It was just a tent next to the chapel, those were the only two buildings there, and outside was a water buffalo. The water buffalo served three purposes: you could get water to drink in your mess cup, fill up your canteens, and then wash your mess gear after you were done eating. The mess gear, consisting of a covered bowl with cutlery inside, was to be carried with you at all times. The food wasn't bad at the mess hall, but in 120-degree weather, it took a while to get used to even wanting to eat.

Before the first operation, a full-scale assault against the North Vietnamese Army (NVA) in helicopters, we would have to run ambushes and set up listening posts in areas to the front of the kill zone. Each night, we had passwords so when we came back into the lines that night or next morning, our own guys would not shoot us. We would get a call to go see Sergeant Wenger, and he would assign different fire teams to set up either ambushes or listening posts. The listening posts usually went out about a half mile, and they were more or less bait. If they heard anything coming, such as a frontal assault, they would have to open fire on the enemy, giving the rest of the line ample time to prepare for the incoming assault. They would be dead in seconds.

The ambush fire team was another story. You would have to go out after dark and go to a predesignated site along a trail or wood line to set up a three- or four-man ambush site. You would have a radio and about five magazines of twenty rounds of M14 ammo (7.62 NATO rounds) and two grenades each. The first thing Mike taught me about ambushes was that they were bullcrap. He said this because we have three guys out there with a total of three hundred rounds and six grenades. What if four hundred enemies come through our ambush site? What we did, and I am not ashamed of, was we would go just past the site of the listening-post guys and wait about forty minutes before calling in that we were at the ambush site. We would be pretty safe there. Then the next morning, we would go back into base camp, and no one was the wiser, except all of the other squads that did the same thing, but we just didn't talk about it.

Time back at the bunker went by incredibly slowly, and you were on edge all of the time. You went to the bathroom right outside of your bunker using an entrenching tool to dig a hole. If you needed to pee, you just did. At night, you would be alone while your foxhole buddy slept. Again, you watched for one and a half hours, slept for one and a half hours, and then repeated the same thing until 6:00 a.m.

It was extremely difficult to stay awake, and you did anything you could to pass the time, but the worst thing was the sounds. It would be highly possible for the NVA to crawl, camouflaged, up to your bunker and get behind you, slitting your throat before you even knew they were there, and then infiltrate the command post behind you. This was always a fear. There were also animals everywhere. Tigers, mongoose, large rats, baboons, and who knows what else made some of those noises. I don't know how many times we would suspect enemy coming through the barbed wire, and grenades would fly, claymore mines went off, and firing would start on the line, only to discover we had killed several mongooses. I remember on an ambush site one night this happened, and we found baboons riddled with bullets.

You would be scared to death that the NVA was sneaking up on you, that a tiger was ready to eat you for lunch, or a deadly snake was just inches away from you, ready to strike at any moment. All the while, you had ten thousand mosquitoes trying to suck your blood. They were as big as planes and would swarm all around your face and body all night, trying to get through your mosquito net worn on top of your helmet, stretching down to your neck. You would button your sleeves and put on mosquito repellent, but with the bites you would get, you would think they actually liked the stuff. Then there were the leeches. I hate leeches to this day. They would climb inside your trousers and suck your blood until they exploded. You would think you had been shot as there was so much blood on your trousers.

You welcomed the chance to get some sleep, but you had to totally trust the person you were with. If he went to sleep on watch, you could both be dead. I will give Sergeant Saxon credit for this one hard rule: if he found you asleep on watch, you would pay big time. I think the primary reason he enforced this was that if we went to sleep and the NVA got past us, he would get his throat slit because he was sleeping about fifty yards behind us.

I remember only one time he had to enforce his rule. There was a black guy named Moss. I really liked Moss, and he was a good guy. But he went to sleep one night on watch. Sergeant Saxon would quietly get within about ten feet of you and whisper the password. If you didn't reply, he would say it louder. If you were asleep, he would grab onto you and your weapon before you could shoot him. Moss fell asleep one night, and he was given the choice of being court-martialed or being beaten. Moss chose the beating. We heard him screaming as he was hit again and again and again.

The next morning, we saw him at sick bay, and he didn't have any black skin on his face; he was all pink. Sergeant Saxon had hit him so many times it ripped the skin right off his face. Moss never complained because he knew he was a fool for falling asleep, but I bet he wished he would have taken the court-martial. Needless to say, no one went to sleep on watch after that.

We always knew when we were going to go on an operation, even before it was announced. We would get replaced on the line by the air wingers. They would cover our positions while we were gone. We would get called back behind the front line, be given a good hot meal, and were allowed to sleep all night. We knew the next morning at 5:00 a.m. we would saddle up and be on choppers to who knows where. We would not know where we were going or what we were doing until we were in the air with our squad. We were usually in the air for about an hour. Some guys would sit on their helmets to protect against possible rounds shot up from the ground. They acted as though it would protect their butts, but a round would go right through a helmet. A helmet was a false sense of protection, it might deflect some shrapnel, but a bullet would go right through it.

When we went on an operation, the weight we had to carry was unbelievable. You would have your regular uniform, boots, helmet, web gear—which you attached everything to—a canteen or sometimes two, nine magazines of twenty rounds each, four grenades, your bayonet, usually another knife, and a backup pistol of some sort to offer you the peace of mind of knowing if you ran out of ammo, you had six rounds to do yourself in instead of being captured. Then you had to carry your meals for a minimum of three days, your mess kit, heat tabs, extra socks and underwear, and another uniform. I didn't wear any underwear over there; it was one less thing to carry. Then you had to carry extra items for the support staff: usually two mortar rounds and possibly a base plate for them, two hundred-round belts of ammo for the machine-gun team, extra batteries for the radios, a LAW, extra rounds for your squad leaders, and an M79 grenade launcher. You also had a first-aid kit, a poncho, and a blanket. If I am forgetting anything, the guys who were there will surely remind me because the weight of all this stuff was unbelievable, especially when you were on a forced march for eight to ten hours a day in the blazing 120-degree weather.

OPERATION HASTINGS

I remember the first operation well. It was in March of 1966. Operation Hastings. I had been in Vietnam for about three months, and the old guys who were there originally had about two months to go before they went back to the States. They were called short-timers and every day reminded me I still had ten months to go. G-2/7 was on many operations while in Vietnam. I don't know the names of the ones they were on before I arrived, but the ones I remember being on were Hastings, Harvest Moon, Prairie One and Two, Double Eagle One and Two, and about five others I didn't know the names of. Usually they were one to three weeks long, and you were in the field or the jungle the entire time.

It was on that first Operation Hastings that I was introduced to World War II C rations. Yes, I said World War II. They were left over from the war, and the USMC never let anything go to waste. Most of the C rations I ate in 1966 were from 1944. They were in a cardboard box and usually contained crackers, gum, cigarettes (usually Lucky Strike or Camels), with four in the pack. You also had instant coffee with cream and sugar packets, a meal, and a dessert. I remember ham loaf, ham and lamas, pound cake, pears, and about four other meals that you could get. You had no choice in which one you got, unless you had the opportunity to steal a case of C rations and take what you wanted.

I loved pound cake and pears. In the beginning, I would trade my cigarettes for pound cake and pears. I would eat my meal, then take the larger can and put the pound cake into the can with the pears and mix them all together, and it was surprisingly good. When we were back at the base camp, I would also trade my two beers a day for the three sodas that everyone got. I got three for two every time, a pretty good deal because at that time, I didn't drink either.

There were also heat tabs to heat up your meal if you had the chance. Most of the time, we were not allowed to have any fires, and even the guys who smoked would cup the cigarette in their palms to keep from getting shot by a sniper at night. The way you would cook your food would be to gather several large rocks and put the heat tab in the middle. Then you open your food with a PR39, the small razor-sharp can opener that you wore around your neck on your dog tag. You would leave a little uncut so you could have a handle on the can. You would then place the can over the heat tab, and voila, instant cooking stove. When we didn't have heat tabs, we would ask the demolition guys for some of their C4.

I remember getting in line at 5:00 a.m. with more marines than I had ever seen. A 6-by truck had picked us up right outside of Sergeant Wenger's tent and transported us down to the airstrip, where several helicopters were sitting with their blades turning slowly.

Why Were We There?

We were taken to areas where each squad was assigned to a certain chopper. I remember Mike saying to me, "Stay close and don't get away from where I am at, and you will be okay. Just keep your head down."

I remember taking my Bible out of my pocket and starting to read. Sergeant Saxon looked at me and said, "Morgan, it is a little late for that. If you didn't have faith before you got here, you won't get it before you get snuffed."

We took off from the airstrip. I was probably as white as a sheet because Sergeant Wenger told us we were headed into some deep s——— in the Quang Tri Province, north of Chi Li and south of Dong Ha, probably about fifty miles south of the river, which separated north and south Vietnam. We were in the air for about an hour. Right before we landed, Sergeant Saxon told us to lock and load because we may get fired upon when we landed. This meant we were going in hot. You took a full magazine, put it into your rifle, and chambered a round. You still had the safety on, but all you had to do was flip the safety off, and you were ready to fire.

We were trained to spread out in a circle around the chopper as soon as we hit the ground. This was not what happened this time. We were over rice paddies, and the choppers could not land. They hovered about ten feet above the ground while we jumped into the rice paddy. We sank to our knees. It was nearly impossible to clean yourself of the muck. I landed in the corner of a rice paddy, and Mike was right beside me. He looked at me and said, "You know what you just landed in?

This is the corner of the rice paddy. That's where the gooks take a s———."

I thought, *Welcome to Vietnam.*

I came out of the rice paddy covered in leeches. Most of the guys smoked, and I soon realized why they did. Several of the old salts ran to me and started lighting up cigarettes, using them to burn the leeches off me. A leech will bury its head into your skin and start sucking; the other end is how they breathe. The guys took the lit cigarette and touched it to the flapping end, making the leech let go because it couldn't breathe. Mike asked me if I wanted a cigarette. I said I had never smoked and didn't want to start.

"You will," he told me.

The operation was to corner a battalion of NVA into a squeeze and wipe them out from the north as they came up from the south. As soon as we started from the landing zone, a Vietcong popped up and started running. I remember the guy who casually lifted his rifle and fired a burst of automatic rounds into the Vietcong's back. His body just exploded, and down he went down in a ball. Everyone tensed, waiting to see more of them, but that was the only one in the area. I remember the guy saying, "Scratch one, zipperhead." I am not proud of the names we called the NVA and the Vietcong, but after you read this, I think you will know why we called them that at that time. There was so much hatred we developed over there, and I am sure the Vietcong hated us just the same.

On that first operation, I really started thinking, *What the hell are we doing here?* It only got worse, reaching a point of hating President Johnson for sending us over there. And for what? I still do not know! I started understanding why we were there the first night of the operation when we were resupplied by helicopter. They brought in tons of ammo and grenades, which we could not carry. There was no food brought in, but there were cases and cases of ammo, batteries, mortars, and more. We were fully loaded when we left the base camp, so we couldn't possibly carry more. We asked what we should do with all of it, and the word came back to just bury it. I probably buried over two million dollars worth of ammo and munitions while I was in Vietnam. The older guys said this happened on every operation. We were in Vietnam not to save South Vietnam from communism but to feed the US war machine, helping factories and bigwigs get rich. To this day, I believe this was the reason we were there, and it makes me sick a thousand times over to know how many guys died for this. I saw right away the South Vietnamese people didn't want us there.

The first day, we didn't meet with much resistance, and the line of troops was spread out over a mile in single file. To protect the main element, you had a point man, a rear security, and flankers. The point man was out by himself. Unless the company commander decided on a double point, then you would have two men who were about thirty yards ahead of the rest of the unit, keeping an eye out for any booby traps. Also if there was a sniper, the point would be taken out, but it alerted the rest of the unit that they had made contact. The rear security was the last man. He watched for enemies approaching from the rear. Again, he would be the first one hit, but it alerted the rest of the unit. The flankers, either right or left, were spread out about two hundred yards from each other. Their job was to let the unit know if there was an ambush set up. Again, you would get killed first, but it would alert the rest of the unit to an incoming attack on the right or left flank.

Later on, I was point or rear security on almost every operation after the old guys transferred back home. For this operation, Mike and I were assigned right flank. The worst thing about flank duty was you had to run through thick jungle, encountering a number of things that would slow you up. Then you had to run and catch up with the rest of the unit. I remember at about two in the afternoon, Mike and I felt like we were ready to die from running to keep up with full gear and our 14-pound rifles. We were dead on our feet, and we didn't know where we were in relation to our platoon. I was sure we were not making it out of there alive. We were lost. We came out of the jungle after being cut to pieces by elephant grass, a plant with leaves like razors. The worst thing about these cuts was that any cut you got over there got infected.

Eventually we came into a clearing. We froze. Before us was a large camp for the NVA, fires still burning with food cooking over them. Tents and gear were all over the place. Fortunately the place had been deserted. I saw a shrine for Buddha. I was just miserable enough about being there, already hating the country and the NVA and everything about them, I took my rifle butt and smashed the shrine. I immediately regretted that decision; it started raining in a downpour, and it rained for two straight days. I never smashed another shrine for Buddha again.

After we cleared the camp, we had to get to someone to report what we had seen, but we didn't have a radio on flank security. We came out of the clearing right into a full squad of marines who almost shot us. It was very close to the command post where the captain was. I remember him demanding, "Who is your platoon sergeant?" Not a second after we answered, he got on his radio and said, "Sergeant Wenger, I have two of your troops here who are supposed to be on flank security. What should I do with them?"

I heard Sergeant Wenger tell him, "Keep them, I don't want them."

We hurriedly told the captain about the deserted camp. That turned out to be incredibly important information. It's what saved our butts.

The captain told us to sit and wait on the side of the trail until our platoon caught up to us. I remember when Sergeant Wenger finally came up the trail. The look he gave us would make your blood run cold. He didn't say anything to us at all; he didn't have to. We fell into formation and were taken off flank guarding that day, thank God!

The next day was the second worst day of my life, and moments from it have haunted me in nightmares for years. I was about to be glad Doc McKeen was with us that day. Doc was the only name we ever called him. He was a baby-faced navy corpsman who had to survive around a bunch of hard-core marines. He didn't take crap from any of us and put us in our place more than once. He was kind, caring, and dedicated to his job, but he could not handle whiners or complainers. He sacrificed carrying extra food and canteens for us on many operations. He was always there hounding us about taking our salt pills every few hours and to stay hydrated. I know many times I saw him give water to a marine who had run out and was hurting. Many more guys would have died on the battlefield if Doc had not been there.

That day, we marched half of the day with sporadic sniper fire and return fire. We had killed several NVA and Vietcong. Many troops had stepped on land mines, booby traps, and Bouncing Betties, which were mortars that would fly into the air about ten feet before exploding and killing everything within a ten-yard radius. I don't know how many guys we lost, but many body bags were flown in. The marines were wrapped in the bag and flown out along, with any wounded. I didn't understand until about six months later why the marines who were seriously but not mortally wounded left smiling. They knew it would get out of this hellhole. It was their ticket home.

That afternoon, we came across a full battalion of ARVINs, the South Vietnamese Army that we were supposed to be fighting for. They wore brand-new gear and looked like they had never been in combat. We were filthy and had our clothes hanging off us after being in the jungle for three days. What I saw was an entire army huddled behind a rice paddy dike, refusing to go forward. We found out there was a full regiment of NVA on the other side of the rice paddy, about three hundred yards away, and the ARVINs were so afraid to go beyond the first set of dikes they were all shaking and muttering to themselves. We walked over the top of them in disgust. The only thing I was afraid of was that they would shoot us in the back, but they didn't. I remember one who spoke English saying it was crazy for us to go toward the enemy, suggesting instead we stay there with them.

We started to move across the rice paddy, and all hell broke loose. Rounds started flying, mortars started going off, and I remember Sergeant Wenger shouting at us to get to the tree line as fast as we could. We were firing from the hip at an unknown assailant who was in the approaching wood line. I saw several guys blown up with mortars and several hit, but we couldn't stop for anything. The firing was too thick.

I remember getting to the wood line and starting to go through. On my right, I heard a gunshot. I looked, and there was a Vietcong strapped to a tree, shooting at the marines behind me. He didn't see me or Mike, who was right beside me. We both opened up and cut him up pretty bad. I remember him just hanging there in the tree. He was a sacrifice for the NVA to slow us down. We continued under heavy fire, and we continued shooting into the wood line where the fire was coming from. I have no idea how many NVA I hit, but we later were told we had killed a thousand NVA that day. The battle was too close for air support, so we couldn't call in any help.

I remember Mike being ten feet away from me, beside me to my rear. The next thing I knew, I heard a *whump*. I felt as though someone had hit me in the back with a sledgehammer. We were wearing flak jackets, and I later found out it was the only thing that saved my life. That and Mike taking a direct hit. I remember flying into the air and smacking down onto the ground again.

I yelled for Mike. There was no answer. I felt a dull pressure in my thigh and my right ankle. I tried to get up and couldn't. I remember Doc McKeen coming to me. I said to him, "Doc, don't worry about me. I'm a goner. My whole back is blown away!"

He rolled me over and told me I would live. My flak jacket was riddled with shrapnel, but it didn't penetrate. I did have several pieces of shrapnel in my ankle and thigh, though. I remember asking about Mike, and Doc just shook his head. "Jack, he took a direct hit. That is the only thing that saved you."

I started looking over my body. I had chunks and pieces of Mike grafted into my clothes and skin from the hot blast. Mike had taken one in the side, and when it exploded, he literally disintegrated. Later, in the medical evacuation (or medevac), they had to take tweezers and pick his body off mine before they operated on me.

I remember my rifle being thrown from my hand, and I never saw it again. It didn't matter because, if I remember correctly, I was out of ammo anyway. I had another hundred rounds in my pack, but by the time I got my magazines loaded, the battle would have been over. I remember blowing several holes with grenades before I got hit. Later, I was told they found an arm and a leg of Mike, and that was all that was sent home.

The fighting was still going strong when two marines came and took me to the rear rice paddy dike, where there were many dead marines. The wounded marines were waiting to be medevaced. Rounds were going over our heads and slapping into the dike, but there was nothing I could do. I couldn't walk. There was a marine beside me who was still alive, but just barely. He must have been a radio operator because he had a .45 pistol in his hand.

I looked down, and they had stripped off his trousers to check his wound. His testicles and penis were gone; he had taken a .50 caliber right in the groin. He was bleeding profusely, and there was nothing to be done for him. He was in horrible pain. I stuck a morphine needle into him. I asked him if there was anything that I could do for him. What happened next, I have lived with my entire life.

He said, "I have lost my dick and my balls, what do I have to live for?" He handed me his .45 pistol and said, "Do me."

At first, I didn't understand, and then I realized he wanted me to kill him because he couldn't do it. He was asking me to kill him! He knew he was going to die. I said a really quick prayer, asking God to help me out in this terrifying situation because I didn't know what to do.

All of a sudden, a peace came over me even though there was fighting going on all around. I looked around.

No one was watching, and no one would know. I took the gun and placed it to the man's temple. I was squeezing the trigger. The marine looked at me, smiled, and dropped his head. He had died before I had to pull the trigger. I have asked myself a thousand times, if he had not died, would I have been able to squeeze the trigger to kill him. Thanks be to God I didn't have to pull the trigger.

They loaded the dead marine and me, alongside five others who were dead, onto the helicopter. The helicopter started lifting off, and one guy started slipping out the door. I looked at the door gunner. Just about when he was grabbing the falling marine, some NVA who had gotten behind the lines opened up on our chopper. Rounds started flying all over the place. Guys who were dead took many of the rounds, but rounds were glancing off grenades still on them and going around inside the chopper. The door gunner opened up with his M60 machine gun that was mounted just forward of the door. He got hit and went down. The chopper finally lifted off, and the rounds quit bouncing around inside of the chopper, but the dead marine started to slip out of the door. I reached over and grabbed onto him and grabbed onto something inside the chopper (I don't remember what) and held on. Eventually one of the crew members helped me get him back into the chopper.

I still relive that day: Mike getting killed, me getting hit, almost killing another marine myself, and then the thought that I would have dropped another marine from the air if he would have fallen from the chopper. That was not a good day.

I remember as we took off looking back and seeing a mortar hit right where the chopper had been. They had zeroed in on us, but we took off in time.

When I got to the med station at Da Nang, I had to wait a long time because there were dozens of guys more seriously wounded than I was. When I finally got to surgery, they didn't have any anesthesia left, so the doctor had to start digging the shrapnel out from my ankle, leg, and temple. The piece of shrapnel in my ankle was a miracle. It had missed bone and tendons. It went in one side and was just sticking out on the other side, being held by skin. The doctor had to go all the way through, however, removing pieces of boot and sock that had penetrated with the shrapnel.

I was put in the hospital for two weeks while I recuperated. It was nice, being there away from combat and the heat and the leeches and the snakes. This lasted for four days until the entire base came under attack. They were infiltrated by Vietcong that had satchel charges with them. A satchel charge is a bag with a high explosive in it that is detonated much like a grenade. There's a pin they pull to ignite the fuse, and then they throw it. It causes extreme damage due to the amount of explosives inside.

The first thing I remember was the corpsman getting everyone out of bed and onto the floor. The lights went out, and .50-caliber rounds started coming through the metal hospital ward about chest high. Then I heard a corpsman at the door about ten feet from my bed scream out as he fired his .45 pistol. I discovered later that a Vietcong had reached the door of our ward and was getting ready to throw a satchel charge inside our ward, but the corpsman had shot him before he pulled the pin. Couldn't we have just a short little break from combat? The infiltration was over when all of the Vietcong were killed. I heard there were about fifty of them that got inside the lines. That was the only time I was at the hospital that we were attacked. The rest of the two weeks were spent relaxing in my bed, reading and eating good hot food.

The coolest thing that happened while I was in the hospital was when Ann Margaret and Johnny Rivers came to Da Nang to put on a show. I couldn't get out of bed yet, and I was pretty bummed, but right after the show, some MPs came through to tell us Ann Margaret and Johnny Rivers were coming through the ward to see us before they leave. We were told to behave ourselves and not to attack Ann Margaret. They were serious. They were actually afraid we would attack Ann Margaret on the ward!

I remember lying in my bed, and here she came. I had not seen an American girl for several months now, and she was beautiful. She still had on the skintight tights from her show, and she came to every bed and said something to each of us. She came and sat on my bed and held my hand, and she asked, "And what happened to you?"

I remember trying to speak, but all that came out was "Ahhh." I tried again, and all that came out was "Ahhh." She started laughing and moved onto the next bed. Johnny Rivers just patted me on the shoulder in understanding; boy, did I feel like an idiot.

BACK AT CHU LAI

After I was released from the hospital, I was right back at it. They put me onto a chopper, and back to Chu Lai I went. One particularly memorably thing happened at Chu Lai. I recall a hot day on the perimeter guarding the airstrip that I was in the bunker on duty with another marine. We heard a helicopter approaching and thought it would be another inspection or some bigwig wanting to come to the front line and talk to the troops. What we didn't know was that John Wayne had been at the airstrip at Chu Lai doing a USO show. We were not allowed to go because of our guard duty. We found out later that John Wayne had asked to go see some of the guys on the lines who could not come to the show. He had been advised not to do this because it was not safe for him, and anything could happen on the front lines at any time. He demanded to go to the front lines, so they took him.

I remember the chopper landing right behind our bunker, with dust blowing everywhere. We didn't know what was going on until this huge man got out of the chopper and started our way. We went out to greet him, and I could not believe my own eyes. It was John Wayne. Real and in person. And he had come to see us. He was really cool, and we talked for about twenty minutes. He thanked us for being dedicated Americans and for what we were doing for the Vietnamese people. Then he told us to keep up the good work, and may God watch over us and keep us safe so we can return home. He shook my hand, and that is a moment I will never forget. His hand was huge, it enveloped mine, and I was in awe of him. John Wayne is now dead, but he will always be my hero, and I know every marine who ever served in the armed forces feels the same. John Wayne was someone we could look up to. He was a great patriotic man dedicated to the armed forces. I thought back to his words many times while in Vietnam.

Returning to Chu Lai after time spent in the hospital was nice. It was good to see the guys; I was issued all new equipment and a new rifle. We went on another operation, but nothing really significant occurred that I can remember, except Bobby Montgomery stepping on a booby trap, after which he had to be medevaced. The other thing I remember was hearing about my best friend from boot camp, Butch Miller, getting killed. I heard he stepped on a land mine, and it killed him instantly. On that operation, there was a lot of fording rivers, and they were very strong. The current was fast, and you had to be extremely careful, especially with all of that weight. One guy tripped and went down. The current got him. We tried to save him, but he got taken away, and we later heard he had drowned.

In one operation, we came up on a large village. Immediately we were under fire. It was terrible; there was no place to hide. When you hear the sound *phew*, that means the round came within eight to ten inches of your head. I heard *phew, phew, phew* so many times I cannot count them. We assaulted the village and killed everything that was there. The Vietcong and villagers were shooting at us. We used the M79 grenade launcher and blew most of the village to bits. Thankfully there were no women or children caught in the line of fire. That was not always the case.

We found a huge weapons cache in the village, and when we finally burned the village to the ground, there were secondary explosions of weapons and ammo for twenty minutes. We burned so many villages that Sergeant Wenger dubbed us Zippos Raiders, after the Zippo lighter we all carried strapped down with a piece of rubber on our helmets. We also found a huge cache of rice meant for the NVA. We called in helicopters and transported the rice back to our base for the friendly village there.

We moved from that village to a village by the South China Sea. That was eye-opening. The people of this village were very tall and stocky, not like the rest of the South Vietnamese people we were used to seeing. We discovered their diet was not rice, like the other areas we had been in; they ate fish. This village was more primitive, and I don't think they had ever seen a white man before. It was funny. They thought we were gods, and fell down and bowed to us. They brought us chairs to sit in, fanned us, and brought us bananas and other fruit. The really funny thing was when they saw the first black guy. They rubbed his skin to see if it would come off, and then they fell down and started worshipping him.

That night, we set up positions on the beach and were told it was quite possible we would be attacked from the ocean with NVA in boats that night. We piled rocks waist high and waited all night, but nothing happened. The next morning, there was a rocky area where you could see when the tide went out. The entire village paraded out at about 6:00 a.m. and went out into the water where the men, women, and children just squatted down and started going to the bathroom. We discovered later this was their restroom. It effectively kept their village sanitary because the ocean would wash away the waste. After they were done, they just huddled together, waiting for us to do the same. We went out onto the rocks and did our morning constitutional. The women just started giggling and laughing. I never could figure why they were laughing at us.

We left the village and got into several small firefights, but nothing significant. The Vietcong would leave men behind as sacrifices, tying them to trees so they could open fire on us when we approached. They usually succeeded in killing or wounding several of our guys before we would kill them. I remember on one trail we came across, the NVA had killed about ten marines. They had cut their heads off and put them on stakes for us to see. Underneath their heads was a sign in misspelled English that said "F—— you, marines!" Needless to say, we were pretty upset about this. Later that day, the rear of the company captured a prisoner. He was passed up the line to where the captain was. I remember seeing he had been bayoneted several times by marines along the way. My squad did not do this, but many others did. When the prisoner got to the captain, he was dead. Nothing was ever said about that ever again.

On that day, we had been in a rice paddy for a long while just before we came up on a village. I remember crossing into the wood line with my fire team and four guys from another platoon. These were still the hard-core guys who had now been in Vietnam for about a year. They had a young Vietnamese girl down on the ground, and they were getting ready to rape her. I stopped them, threatening to shoot them if they didn't get up and leave. Finally they did.

Why didn't I report the guys for stabbing the prisoner and the guys who were about to rape a young girl? The answer is simple: I wanted to stay alive. When you wanted to live, you didn't rat out on anyone for anything. I did my best to stop things that happened around me, and that was all I could do. I still have a clear conscience about what I did over there because it was war, and I kept it at that.

One operation shortly after this one turned out to be an amazing logistics feat. We had to surround a large village, where we had been told many Vietcong were. They had taken over the village, killed the village chief, and we pretty well dug in. Our job was to wipe them out and save as many villagers as possible. We started our attack and received gunfire immediately. We ducked for cover behind an immense rice paddy dike surrounding the village. After we called in helicopter support, they used their grenade pods and M60 machine guns to take down the Vietcong firing at us. With air support, we returned fire with M79 grenade launchers and the bazooka-like LAWs some carried slung over their shoulders.

We assaulted the village when the fire lightened up and encountered several Vietcong were still alive after our initial fire. We then started searching for villagers, whom we found in holes all over the village. Some of the holes had Vietcong in them, and we had to drop grenades in them to clear them out. Some villagers got killed that day, but it was unavoidable. I cannot remember how many Vietcong we had killed that day, but there were many. They had been using the village as a food supply for their soldiers due to its large rice cache. We now understood why the village was so important to hit: without it, the Vietcong could not operate in this area. They had done unimaginable things to the villages. I could not understand it. It was their own people they were hurting.

We swept the entire village and rounded up all of the elderly, women, and children. There were no young men in the village because the Vietcong had recruited them into the army, offering them no choice but to fight. There was a village several miles away where the villagers we rounded up would be safe at. A huge airlift was started. The villagers were told they had to take with them everything they could carry, and then we put them onto helicopters and took them to their new home. Many of them did not want to go, but we knew after we left, anyone left in the village would be killed by the Vietcong. We also put all of the cached rice into drums and containers to load onto helicopters for the villagers. This venture took almost two days, and the entire time, we had a perimeter set up to guard against an attack.

When everyone was gone, choppers came in to pick us up. It got down to the last chopper, and there was just myself and Graham left. There was not enough room on the chopper, and we were told another chopper would pick us up in about fifteen minutes. This was not my idea of a good time. We were hundreds of miles from anywhere familiar, out there by ourselves, and the Vietcong could come back at any moment. This was one of the most frightening experiences during the entire time we were in Vietnam. Finally, about fifteen minutes later, an army Huey Cobra landed about twenty feet from us. They told us to get in quick because Vietcong had been spotted in the area. We lifted off right away. Once we were in the air, we spotted them in the jungle headed for the location we had just left. The chopper team asked if we didn't mind going on an airstrike with them. We said, "Go for it!"

They sighted on the Vietcong and lowered the Cobra. They started firing all of their missile pods and machine guns at them. It was unbelievable what that chopper could do. This was the first and only time I ever rode on a Cobra, and it was amazing.

As time went on, we eventually lost all of the hard-core guys who had been there for their thirteen-month tour. We started getting in replacements for them, all of which were totally raw, just out of boot camp. They all looked to me and Lopez for training. The worse thing that occurred was we got a new squad leader. I will not say his name because you will find he did many things later on that can be verified by the guys in my squad.

Sergeant Wenger did not leave with the other troops, choosing to sign on for another thirteenth-month tour, and thank God he did. Sergeant Wenger was a hard man, and if you messed up, he was right on top of you with severe punishment, but he was fair, he was a warrior, and he had no fear. He carried a .45, and I never saw it out of the holster. He was always there for us directing fire, telling us what to do every time there was a firefight or operation. He cared about us, and I will never forget him.

We finally got a lieutenant to be our platoon commander, and Sergeant Wenger reverted back to being platoon sergeant. The new lieutenant was a total idiot. We got a new captain, and he was fantastic. He was smart, well educated in warfare, and stayed cool under pressure. I also remember being in awe of how well he kept himself in top physical condition.

The guys we were getting in as replacements were draftees, and I really felt sorry for them. I had joined voluntarily out of high school, but while I had been there for four months, the United States had initiated the draft. The guys we got in did not want to be there, and some were directly out of jail. Judges back in 1966 were setting a sentence on with a choice: either go to jail or join the Marine Corps. Many opted to go to the Marine Corps. Lopez, Bobby Montgomery, and I trained and mentored McGee, an atheist from Illinois, and a mean quiet black guy from Detroit. He always said that if he made it out alive, he wanted to be a Detroit police officer. There were several guys from the Philippines and Mexico too.

Three of my best friends, even to this day—Bobby Donaldson, Bob Pabst, and Cecil Covel—were with me on many patrols and operations. Bobby was a machine gunner while Cecil and Bob were in my fire team. Cecil was married and worked his farm in Oklahoma before he was drafted. I couldn't believe we were drafting guys that were married and running a farm, leaving his wife to handle everything. Bob Pabst joined and was a really good soldier, as were Cecil and Bobby.

Graham and I were foxhole buddies and endured many an operation. We were usually the point men or rear security. As I stated before, the point men usually did a single or double point and were the first ones who made contact with the enemy. We were trained in booby traps, and I discovered many before anyone was hurt, but on two occasions, I blew it.

The first one was when I was on an operation and walking a single point. There was a punji pit that had been on this trail for many, many years. That was the only thing that saved me. I didn't see it because it was so well covered with years of vegetation grown over it. I fell about ten feet into the pit. Fortunately, the stakes were rotted due to the time they had been there, and I just crashed through them and landed on my back. The problem was that landing on my back meant landing on a full pack and entrenching tool. I hurt my back pretty badly, and I still have problems with it to this day, but I survived.

Another time, I was walking point again, and I felt my foot hit a wire. I knew what it was immediately, and I had not seen it. When I tripped on the wire, I froze and yelled, "Booby trap!" I was hoping those behind me would have time to hit the ground before it went off. I knew I was a goner, and my life flashed before my eyes. I stood waiting, and nothing happened. The guys behind me fanned out and found the Bouncing Betty. It was sitting in the ground just off the trail about six feet. The Vietcong who had put it in the ground had forgotten to straighten out the pin so it would pull loose, activating the blasting mechanism on the Betty. God was with me so many times in Vietnam I cannot count them.

On another operation, I was rear security for a company-sized operation. The Vietcong had a habit of leaving behind one of their men for a suicide mission. They would dig a hole to create what I described earlier as a spider trap, where the man would hide and wait for us to go by before springing up behind us to attack. This was meant to be more of a demoralizing attack than anything, but it worked on many occasions, and we lost a lot of men. I remember constantly looking around to see if anything was coming up on our rear, and I had just turned halfway when I felt a hot sting on the side of my face, followed by the sound of a gunshot. The VC had popped up about fifteen feet away from me and meant to hit me on the head, but when I turned, the round grazed my cheek.

There was a machine gun team in front of me, and the gunner carried his M60 in a jungle sling. He immediately swung around and opened up on the VC. The VC was about half out of the hole, and I remember the gunner shot him so many times his body almost separated at the waist. I wore a bad blister on my cheek where the round just barely broke the skin for about a month.

OPERATION DOUBLE EAGLE

The heat was unbearable, and the nights were cold. I remember on one operation, Double Eagle, we were in the jungle for about a week. Three things happened that week to make my hair stand on end. We would be choppered into an area on every operation. On this one, they said the landing zone would be hot. This meant that they were dropping us right in the middle of a large detachment of NVA. We were told planes had gassed the entire area with tear gas to confuse the enemy, so we could land and get a perimeter set up for the rest of the choppers coming in. We put on gas masks in 120-degree heat, and it was sweltering, but when we landed and exited the chopper, we were glad we had them on. The tear gas was like a thick fog, and when we hit the ground, we were under heavy fire. Rounds were flying everywhere while we worked to set up a perimeter and start laying down a field of fire that cleared a circle with a half-mile radius. Our fire was so intense it forced the NVA to draw back, allowing the rest of the choppers to land without much resistance.

We called in an airstrike from a ship many miles away on the retreating NVA. The forward observer that called it in was a little off on his information. We heard the rounds coming in about fifty yards from us. With shrapnel flying all around us, several guys were hit. I heard a whoosh, and then a thud. I looked down at a piece of metal from a bomb that had come flying at me. It was stuck in the ground a foot away from my leg. It would have cut me in half. I remember the squad leader freaking out. He carried his M79 grenade launcher on his belt. When he grabbed for it, he hit the trigger, and the weapon went off, pointing toward the ground. The round stuck in the dirt a few feet from us. Without thinking, we all ran, hit the ground, got up, ran again, and then hit the ground again. We knew we were dead because the grenade in the launcher had a killing radius of ten yards. The thing we forgot about the M79 launcher was that it had a built-in safety, preventing it from arming itself until it had traveled ten yards through the air. It just sat there in the ground smoking and never went off. I remember several guys had to clean out their underwear that morning.

The next hair-raising experience was thanks to a blue snake about six inches long: the bamboo viper. It is one of the deadliest snakes in the word. Its nickname in Vietnam was the three-stepper. Step 1: you get bit. Step 2: you put your head between your legs. Step 3: you kiss your ass good-bye. That was about all of the time you had before the venom paralyzed your entire nervous system, and everything would just shut down.

At night, we would stop for our one and a half hours of sleep and watch cycles. It was rather chilly that one night, and I had the last sleep before everyone awoke at 6:00 a.m. I had rolled up on the ground in my poncho to stay warm. I had been taught by Mike Allen to lie perfectly still when you woke up. You moved very slowly until you were standing up, and then you would shake out your poncho. I did this routine every day, but this day, a bamboo viper had crawled in with me during the night, and when I shook out my poncho, he slithered away.

I lost my breath for a moment and thanked God I had followed Mike's teaching. I hate snakes to this day. The only good snake is a dead snake. My wife once put a fake rubber snake in my medicine closet above the sink, and when I opened the door, it fell out on me. I was so terrified she said she would never do that again, but I still think she has it somewhere in the house. I dread the day it might reappear.

The next day, when we got up, we prepared to force march another ten to fifteen miles. We readied ourselves and put on our helmets, which had been lying on the ground. On that day, I didn't look inside my helmet and just put it on. In the top of the helmet, there is a web liner that protects your head from hitting the top of the helmet. After we marched all day and stopped in a secure area for the night, I took my helmet off and threw it on the ground. Allen was standing beside and startled me with, "Oh my god, Jack, look inside your helmet!"

There I found a ten-inch scorpion hanging upside down between the liner and the top of the helmet. I took my bayonet and stabbed it in the back; the tail hit the bayonet so hard it moved my hand to one side. I kept thinking what if that tail had hit me in the head.

I'm not sure, but I think that would have been fatal. I also do not like scorpions to this day, or spiders or leeches or mosquitoes, for that matter.

The last story about this operation was probably the scariest night of my entire life, and I only tell it because I know now the Marine Corps cannot do anything to me for what we did that night. It has been over forty-seven years now, and I don't think they are interested in me. We were probably sixty miles from anywhere on this operation in the Quang Tri province north of Chu Lai and south of Dong Ha. We had a full battalion operation at that time, and we stopped for the night to set up a perimeter.

When I was called to Sergeant Wenger, he said to get my fire team together and go out about three miles to set up an ambush. I thought, *You have got to be kidding me.* We were out in the middle of nowhere, and he wanted me to take three other men miles into enemy territory? But I never questioned Sergeant Wenger's orders, so I assembled my men, and we started out when it got dark. Our job was to be sacrifices in case the NVA was coming toward the battalion. It would give the rest of the troops an early warning.

We were given three grenades each, water, eight magazines of twenty-round ammo, and a radio. We went out about two miles and found a good trail for the ambush; we were about eight feet off of the trail. I told the guys one of us would keep watch while the other three slept. Then we would switch off during the night. At about 3:00 a.m., I awoke to Graham with his hand over my mouth, and he just pointed to the trail. Before he could do anything, several NVA came through the ambush site at a full run. They were hard-core NVA with brown uniforms and backpacks. The moonlit night showed them very well.

Graham pointed to the right of the trial and, with hand signals, indicated that about fifty had already gone through the ambush site before he woke me up. He sort of raised his shoulders and, with his hands, indicated, "Okay, boss, what do we do now?"

I looked at the other guy sleeping, and knowing we were just a few feet away from hundreds of NVA, I just sat there. I looked at Graham and shook my head no. The NVA were running away from the battalion. If they had been going toward the battalion, we would have had no choice but to open up on them to give the battalion warning. By the time I shook my head no to Graham, another couple hundred NVA had run through the site. I started counting ammo. We didn't have enough ammo to kill all of them, even if we only spent one bullet per man. Nearly a thousand NVA went through our ambush that night.

When the last of them went by and several minutes had passed, Graham asked, "Do we tell the other guys about this?"

I answered him, "No, and we will never speak of this again. This never happened."

If I had it to do over again, I would have done the same thing. An ambush is meant for tens, not thousands. I am truly glad the other guy didn't snore, or fart, in his sleep.

THIRTEEN DAYS AT HOME

We got back to base camp after being in the bush for three weeks and were told we were going out again as soon as we got showers and fresh supplies. Right before we left, I got deathly sick in the morning and went to the sick bay, but they couldn't find anything wrong with me. I got sick again the next morning and had terrible back pain. Again before we left for the operation I was in deep pain. I asked Sergeant Wenger if I could stay back because of being ill. His answer was, "Do you want to let the rest of your platoon down just because you have a tummy ache?" I decided to go on the operation, sick or not.

Right before we left, I received a letter from Barb telling me she was pregnant. She asked if I would want to marry her. I immediately went to Sergeant Wenger, who told me if I didn't want to marry her not to worry about it because the corps will handle it for me. I told him I had to get home to get married because I was going to be a dad. He told me to go to the chaplain, who was a real jerk. I told him about Barb and the baby, and Reverend Pearson said, "Well, I'll see what I can do, but you don't need to be home very long because you have already had your honeymoon." I wanted to punch him, but I kept my cool. I will never forget the smirk on his face. I could have killed him.

Sergeant Wenger said he could not give me an emergency leave, but he would try for an administrative leave that would last about two weeks. I wrote to Barb and told her I loved her and I would do everything I could to get home to get married before our baby was born. At this time, it was the third week of June, and Barb was due in September. I discovered later Reverend Pearson could have given me an emergency leave, but he opted not to do so.

I still had my sickness and pain the entire operation. The operation was a terrible one; we lost many good men to the intense fighting. When I got back, the doctor looked at me again and said, "We cannot find anything wrong with you." He then asked, "Is there any chance your wife is pregnant?" I told him about Barb and that I was trying to get home to get married. He told me to get out and not come back. I had sympathy morning sickness. When I left the doctor, Reverend Pearson was waiting for me with my orders for an administrative leave. My time started immediately, and I had thirteen days to be back before being counted absent without leave (AWOL).

I was eighteen years old, ten thousand miles from home, and I didn't know where to start first. I went to the payroll officer only to find I had $300 in my account. He gave me a check. I had no cash. I didn't even shower or change, I had on clothes that were torn off, I was dirty, sweaty, and tired. I threw some things together and started walking toward the airstrip, still not knowing what to do or how to get home. The captain's jeep driver came by and asked me what was going on. I told him, and he said, "Hop in, and I'll take you to the airstrip." I didn't hesitate because it was twelve miles away. He told me one thing that saved me several days: "When you get down on the runway, there will be a crew chief at one of the C-130s. Hold up your envelope, and tell him you need to get to Okinawa and you have emergency leave papers. They will put you on the first plane out, ahead of anyone. If he asks, tell him you had a death in your family." He told me administrative leave papers don't get you anything, and you would be lucky to get out of the country.

The driver dropped me off at the airstrip where there was a C-130 on the runway with the engine running. I went to the crew chief and told him I needed to get to Okinawa because of a death in the family. I was in luck; the plane was going to Okinawa. He told me to get on. I couldn't believe things were going so smoothly, but that was just the first leg.

I arrived in Okinawa on July 4. Everything was closed, and I didn't have the faintest idea what to do. I asked around, but no flights were going out. I was told where to find a transit barracks I could probably stay at. I got a room, and I needed clothes. We had stored our seabags from the States with our personal stuff in a hanger in Okinawa. It was about ten miles from the barracks, and I didn't know how to get there. I tried to get my $300 check cashed, but no banks were open due to the holiday.

I had no money for a cab, I ate at the mess hall, but that did not get me to the staging area where my seabag was. I remembered my sisters had given me a cashmere sweater, which was worth about $40 even back then, for Christmas. I hailed a taxi driver and told him my situation. I promised him the cashmere sweater if he drove me to get my seabag and back to the transit barracks. He agreed, and I was able to retrieve my seabag there. I arrived back at the transit barracks, showered, and changed into a clean but very musty uniform. I still had my PFC chevrons on the sleeves, and I had been promoted to lance corporal while in Vietnam. I didn't have any ribbons to wear that I had earned, but I didn't care.

I checked with the terminal and advised them I needed to get home right away. They said everything was full, and it would be several days before I could get a flight back to the States. I was on a countdown of thirteen days, and I had already used three. I went to my room at the transit barracks and was pretty down and depressed. I was just sitting there on my bed when another marine entered the room and introduced himself. He said he had just arrived from the States and would be stationed here in Okinawa, but they didn't have a room for him yet. He asked me why I was so down, and I told him about trying to get home to get married. He laughed. I didn't see the humor in it. He then apologized for laughing, but the reason he was laughing was that his new job starting tomorrow was director of the flight line. He said he would get me on a flight first thing in the morning without any problem. I told him it was like God had sent him.

The next morning, I was on a plane for a ten-thousand-mile ride to California. The flight was long and hard; the plane was a troop carrier, and you sat on web seats the entire way, eating meals out of boxes. I didn't care; I was going home. We landed at a base just outside Los Angeles. I checked the flight line for any flights to Dayton, Ohio. There were none. I now had a real dilemma. I was in the States, but Ohio was a long way away. I called Barb and told her I was in California, but I didn't know what to do. She said to go ahead and fly commercial. I went to the airport by cab and was able to cash my check at the airport bank. Luckily, at that time, they had a reduced airfare for servicemen in uniform.

The reservation person at the airport was the only smile I saw on a face the entire time at the airport. No one would speak to me, and most looked at me with disgust. Being a marine in 1966 was not such a respectable thing. Everyone hated the war, they thought of all marines as baby killers, and it was reflected in everyone's body language at the airport and on the plane home. It was like I had some sort of incurable communicable disease.

I thought of everything I had been through—losing friends, getting shot, the heat, the miserable living conditions—and I thought I was doing all this for my country while my country looked at me with disdain. Why do all of these people hate me for trying to do the right thing? I was doing what I thought John Wayne would have done. I still cannot believe the way we were treated when we came home, and it wasn't until about two years ago the first person said to me, "Thanks for what you did in Vietnam." I was so shocked I didn't know how to reply.

I arrived in Dayton, Ohio, and hailed a cab to take me home. I had to look up my parents' new address because the newly constructed US 35 had taken our old house. The city had come through and issued imminent domain and bought the houses in my old neighborhood. My parents moved north of Dayton, and I had never seen the house before. It was pretty sad to come home to find the house I had lived in all my life was nothing but a stretch of highway. I thought of my comic book collection and my baseball cards. I later learned my parents had forgotten them in the attic when they moved. They were all gone—cards and original Batman, Superman, GI Joe, and Archie comics.

I gave the cab driver the address, and he dropped me off at the end of the driveway next to the street. It was early in the morning, and none in my family knew I was coming home yet. My sister, Donna, had a Mustang parked in the driveway, and it was unlocked. I put down my seabag and started blowing her horn. Everyone came outside to see what was going on, and there I stood in the driveway. Emotions ran high, and tears of joy were shared that morning the first week of July 1966.

After meeting with my family for about one hour, I asked my sister if I could borrow her car to go see Barb. She agreed, and I drove to Barb's house. It was about nine in the morning. Again, she didn't know I was home yet. I went to the door and knocked on it. She answered the door and put her hand to her mouth and slammed the door. I couldn't help but think, *Wow! I just traveled ten thousand miles to get married, and my bride-to-be slams a door in my face.*

She opened the door again, and said she was so shocked she did it out of instinct. We hugged and kissed and held each other for a long while. We spent the rest of the day together, catching up with each other. She was showing pretty well, with our baby-to-be born in September. We started making wedding plans and counting the days I had left. I had to allow four days to get back to my unit in Vietnam, so we were down to just a few days to make the wedding plans, get the church booked, notify my immediate family, buy rings, and have a ceremony.

We went to her minister, and he wasn't very happy about the situation, but he agreed to speak with us. When he realized we were in love and I had left Vietnam so our baby would have a name when it was born, he agreed to marry us in two days. Plans were made, and the next day, we went to buy rings. I didn't have much money, so both of our rings cost a total of $300. We were married at Barb's church with our families there to witness and support our love. I will never forget when Barb's grandfather (who had raised her) first showed up for the wedding. He said he didn't know whether to bring flowers or a shotgun, and I think he was serious. My parents had a reception after the wedding at their house. The wedding was short and sweet. I knew I loved Barb with all my heart. We have been together ever since and have had three wonderful children: Chris, Kerry, and Kelli, each with a family of their own now.

We didn't have any money for a honeymoon, so to speak, and didn't have enough time to take one anyway. My brother Paul gave us enough money to travel about thirty miles north of Dayton to Troy, Ohio, where he had made reservations for us at a hotel for one night. That was our honeymoon, but to me, it was the best day of my life, and we loved each other all night.

The next day, when we got home, I called Wright Patterson Air Force Base to see if I could hop a flight back to California. Again I lied and told them I was returning from an emergency leave. They said there was a flight going out the next morning, but that was the last flight for the week. I decided to take the flight. It was a cargo plane. The entire flight was like riding a bus over railroad tracks, but it was a flight.

Before I left, I borrowed money from my dad and bought a huge suitcase to fill to the brim with candy, canned food of all sorts, and anything I thought the guys in my squad would like to have. I also asked my dad if I could have my grandpa's .38-caliber revolver to carry as a backup weapon, and my dad gave it to me. Back then, there were no airport searches, so I put it into my carry-on, and no questions were ever asked. I am glad I brought it with me.

I flew to California, regretfully leaving everyone at home to go back to Vietnam. I kept thinking something really bad was going to happen, and I was correct. It was hardest of all to leave Barb, knowing she would have to deal with her entire pregnancy alone. The worst part I knew was her embarrassment because she was still in high school and wasn't due to graduate for another month. We are still together after forty-seven years.

When I arrived in California at the air base, I inquired about getting a flight back to Vietnam. They were all full, and I was informed I would have to wait two days in the airport for a flight to Saigon. I asked if any flights were going to Chu Lai, where I needed to go. There were none. I didn't have any choice but to get on the list for Saigon. I slept in the airport for two nights using my seabag and suitcase for a pillow. Food was scarce, but I stole some things from the suitcase I was taking back for the guys. I ate cold spaghetti and meatballs and Vienna sausage for two days.

The flight finally arrived, and it was fantastic. It was a Delta commercial flight the government had hired to take guys to Vietnam. The stewardesses were great, and I take off my hat to them for flying into Vietnam because they didn't know what they would encounter. The food on the flight was good, and I slept most of the way. As we neared Saigon, the pilot came over the radio and said, "Hold on, guys, we are doing a fast and angled descent to avoid gunfire."

He was not kidding. He started down, and my stomach went up my throat. It was like riding a roller coaster at 500 mph. We landed without incident. The hardest thing after we landed was lugging around the stuffed suitcase that held all the goodies for the guys in my squad. I told them I would bring back what I could, and I knew they were looking forward to it. The suitcase had to weigh eighty pounds and at today's airport would have cost me more to have it on the plane than what the items inside it were worth.

I got to Saigon with three days to get back to my unit, which was many miles north of Saigon in Chu Lai. I got off the plane, unsure of what to do next. I had no weapon other than my grandfather's .38 pistol, which I had loaded in another bag. I lied again and told someone at the airstrip I had been on an emergency leave and had to get back to my unit in Chu Lai. It had worked for twenty thousand miles of hitchhiking, so why stop now? One guy at the airstrip told me there were no helicopters going out today for Chu Lai, but there would be one in the morning. He said he would get me a seat on it. I asked him where I could stay the night. There was an in-transit barracks about ten miles away from the airstrip for people just like me. He managed to get a jeep to take me there. He said in the morning I would have to get a Vietnamese cab because there wouldn't be anyone available that early in the morning. He cautioned me about the Vietnamese cab drivers; many of them were Vietcong. It was not uncommon for a cab driver to be driving you to a destination and suddenly pull into an alleyway, where the driver would jump out of the cab, leaving you sprayed with bullets or blown to bits by a bomb inside the cab itself.

I was driven to the in-transit barracks and given a bunk to sleep in. There was nowhere to eat, so again, I ate some of the food I had brought for the squad. The good thing is by morning, the suitcase was a little lighter. I woke the next morning after having a restless night. I was in Vietnam, and I didn't have my buddies with me to watch my back, and I did not have my M14. I felt naked without it.

I remembered what the guy on the flight line had told me about using caution with the Vietnamese cab drivers, and I sort of feel guilty for what I did next. I hailed a taxi, and a Vietnamese driver asked me where I wanted to go. I told him the heliport, and we negotiated a price. When we had driven a block from the in-transit barracks, I casually took the .38 revolver out of my bag and told him I wouldn't shoot him as long as he did just what I said. I put the gun to his temple and told him if he deviated from our route I would blow his head off. I asked him if he understood to nod his head. The blood drained from his face, and I saw his knuckles turn white on the steering wheel as he nodded. I arrived at the heliport without incident, and I am sure he was glad to see me leave his cab. I probably didn't have to pay him, but I didn't want to get into any more trouble if he decided to report me. I never heard anything about this incident again, and I am still alive to tell the story, so I think it was a wise decision.

I arrived at the heliport, and we left promptly at 6:00 a.m. The flight was uneventful, and I arrived at Chu Lai two hours later. I was back two days early, before I would be classified as being AWOL, but I still had to get back to my unit, and there was no way that I could walk it. Miraculously, the captain's jeep driver came by and told me to get in, offering to take me to my squad. He had driven to the air base to drop off mail. I thought this is where I started twenty thousand miles and eleven days ago, and now I am back in the same jeep, headed back to my unit. I kept thinking that Reverend Pearson would be disappointed I had made it back on time, and I made sure as soon as I checked in with Sergeant Wenger, I went to the reverend and sarcastically said, "Reverend, thanks for all of your help getting me home." He knew I was being disrespectful, but I made sure I said it in a way he couldn't write me up for anything. I never spoke to him again, and refused to go to his services.

I got back to the squad, and they were overjoyed at what I had brought back for them. We divided up the goodies and ate for several days until we almost got sick. There was another surprise when I got back: my mother had forgotten to tell me she had mailed me a rum cake for my birthday because she was told it was the only thing that would arrive not spoiled. We also ate that in one sitting. She had put too much rum in it, and we were all feeling rather good after that.

I told them about the trip home, the wedding, and especially the honeymoon. They wanted to know every detail. Sorry, Barb, I told them everything! They then told me everything that had happened while I was gone and about the operation they had just returned from. They also said something was up, and there had been rumblings about us moving out in the morning. I got all of my gear reissued and loaded my rifle and pack just in case we needed to pull out at a moment's notice.

OPERATION HASTINGS II

This was a huge operation in which we again were supposed to be landing south of a full division of North Vietnamese. The army was landing north of the site, and together, we would squeeze them in to wipe them out. The NVA had no helicopters, no air support, no tanks, and no good supply lines. We had all of the above. It was supposed to be a turkey shoot; it turned into one of the biggest operations I had ever been on. Thousands of marines in one area, it was unbelievable.

The first encounter we had was on a huge plain. We were wide open, and gunfire was directed toward us. Rounds were flying everywhere. We returned fire at an unseen enemy; all we knew was the fire was coming from a hillcrest we couldn't see anyone on. The fire was so intense we had no choice but to hit the deck with rounds flying over our heads and hitting the ground all around us. The fire increased, and we had no place to look for cover. They had caught us in the open. The most miraculous thing about this day was that although thousands of rounds were fired at us, no one got hit.

The fire stopped, and we went to the top of the hill, with me as point. Down below, in the most beautiful valley I had ever seen, was a village. I saw hundreds of

Vietcong running everywhere, carrying guns. I opened fire on them and hit a few while others around me did the same. What we didn't know was the forward observer had called in Phantoms to hit the village. I can only hope the village didn't have civilians in it because the next thing I knew, a helicopter flew right over our heads and was firing so many rounds at the village the empty casings from the M60 machine guns were falling all around us and actually hitting us. The rounds casings were so hot they burned our arms when they hit us.

Then the most unbelievable thing I had ever seen happened: we heard the Phantoms coming and looked up. A plane flew over so close to our heads, it couldn't have been more than twenty feet above us. I waved to the pilot, and he gave me the thumbs-up as he dropped two napalm canisters on the village.

We knew what would happen next. Right before the bombs hit, we hit the ground. The heat was so intense it felt like our faces were on fire, and we were a fair distance from the impact. A huge red ball of hundred-foot flames erupted, consuming the entire village. There was no doubt in my mind: all of the Vietcong there had been incinerated in an instant.

I wasn't on the cleanup that went through the village. We were told to head a different direction into an open plain, probably three miles square. The pilot of one of the Phantoms called in that he saw something strange from the air. He said it was like dozens of square holes in the ground across the plain.

We approached the first hole and couldn't believe what we saw. The holes were roughly twelve feet twelve square. There were about thirty of them across the plain. There were no dirt piles from digging the holes, it had all been hand carried away. The holes were so deep we couldn't see the bottom. I dropped a smoke grenade down one hole, and it took forever to hit the ground. The grenade went off, and we started seeing smoke coming from the other holes too. This meant they were all connected. The holes had handholds carved into the dirt, creating a ladder. I cannot imagine actually trying to go down into the hole using the indentations that were there. We knew right away we had discovered something huge. We had heard of the underground bases the North Vietnamese had, but this was the first one we had seen. They had many years to do all of this digging, but I cannot imagine the manpower it took to perform this task.

Sergeant Wenger put everyone on alert, but he was curious just how deep the holes were. He told me to drop a grenade down one of the holes, so I pulled the pin and dropped it. We waited seven seconds before the grenade blew, but I don't think it had hit the ground yet. He called up a demolition team and had them set satchel charges for various time delays. They started dropping everything they had into the holes, waiting for something to get to the bottom before exploding.

The satchel charges started blowing underneath us, and smoke was pouring out of holes twenty feet away from the one they dropped the charge in. They even made makeshift C4 bombs with a timer on them and dropped them into the holes. Eventually all of the holes had smoke coming from them, and there was nothing else we could do, except move on cautiously, watching our backs as we left. We thought about calling in an airstrike with B52s, but it would have been useless due to the holes being so deep. To this day, we don't know how many North Vietnamese we killed that day. The area could have housed an entire battalion, possibly the one we were looking for to corner in the squeeze with the army, but we couldn't be sure.

The biggest thing that still baffles me to this day is what they did with all of that dirt. You had the dirt from the hole itself and then the dirt from the tunnels underneath the ground connecting the holes. They were no dirt mounds around for at least half a mile. Each load of dirt had to be hand carried up the holes to the top and then carried away. I cannot imagine one man carrying more than twenty pounds of dirt for the climb and then walking miles away to dump it. It could have been done prior to us arriving there, possibly against the French, but I guess we will never know. I can only hope someone will call me up someday and let me know how this was accomplished.

On the way back to our pickup point, we set up a perimeter, and my squad was ordered to take out a patrol to ensure the hill near the battalion was secure. We were tired and angry and hot and thirsty and hungry. I remember the jungle was really thick, making for a rough trail. We had to climb an incredibly steep hill to get to the top before starting to circle the hill for any signs of NVA. This was probably the best day I had in Vietnam. We came out of the jungle into a densely wooded area.

Suddenly the entire area opened up into the most beautiful spot I have ever seen: lush vegetation, beautiful flowers everywhere, and a stream coming from a waterfall that ran cold and crystal clear. We drank the cold water and took off all our gear to wash ourselves off the best we could. We drank until we couldn't drink anymore, then emptied all our canteens and filled them up with the water. It was the best water I have ever tasted.

In this ten-to-fifteen-minute time we were away from the war, we thought we were in the Garden of Eden. It was the most beautiful thing I have ever seen on this earth. It was as though God had given this moment to us as a break from the hell we had endured for months. I wondered how such a beautiful place could be in such a terrible country. No words can do justice to describing that place.

We left hesitantly, knowing we had to get back to our patrol. We finished the patrol, secured the hill, and eventually arrived back at the battalion with smiles on all our faces and a little more peace than we had set out with.

FIRST OPERATION AT DONG HA

We returned to Chu Lai and ran patrols and ambushes for several days with nothing really happening. We received reports again of something really big going on up north of us. The third day back, we were told to pack up all our gear for a three-week operation. We were told to move to the CP area. We knew this was no false alarm; it was the only time we were allowed to sleep the whole night with no guard duty. We were also concerned when they called for anyone wanting to go to church services that night. We all went. That was the only time in my life I was allowed to take Catholic communion; the Protestant minister was nowhere to be found.

The next morning, we were briefed on the operation. We were going to Dong Ha and then onto a location called the Rock Pile. We didn't even know where Dong Ha was but were told it was really close to North Vietnam in the demilitarized zone. Right away there were rumors of us invading North Vietnam, sweeping north to Hanoi, and bringing Ho Chi Minh to his knees. Then we could go home.

We knew we were not supposed to be in the DMZ, so this was going to be big. Our new squad sergeant told us we were going to load up on trucks and be taken to the air strip. There we would load onto C-130 airplanes and be flown to Dong Ha. We were told to pack everything we were not taking with us and put it into our seabags in storage at Chu Lai. This meant anything and everything we were not carrying for an operation. We wanted to pack as lightly as possible, so we left behind everything we could. Everything I had that was of a personal nature—cameras, photos, and clothing—would never be seen again. We were then given extra ammo, extra grenades, and double the normal food and extra items to carry.

Once we got on the planes and ready to take off, the captain informed us as soon as we landed in Dong Ha, we would be given a quick meal and then we would force march about twenty miles into the DMZ. We would first secure an area for choppers to land then we had to put 105 recoilless rifles, small artillery pieces into place for support of our operation. This would later become an outpost and the location of a huge siege called Con Tien the next year.

We were told as soon as we got the area secured and the artillery in place we would then force march north, where a company of marines were pinned down and had been for several days. They had been on an operation when they were ambushed by the North Vietnamese. Many were dead. I think their unit was Echo Company 2/4, the second battalion, fourth regiment of our same division.

We arrived in Dong Ha and were surprised by the size of the airstrip. It was just one runway with marines for security, but it was mainly air force in the middle of nowhere. We were given a hot meal. Then we started out on a forced march with two or three other companies. We were finally told there was a huge North Vietnamese force in the area, and our job, after we rescued the ambushed marines, was to find out where the North Vietnamese were.

The intense feelings of Sergeant Wenger, our captain and squad leader, were unlike anything I'd seen before. He pushed us to our limit that day. Most of the march was on a dirt road covering many miles. It was extremely hot there, and the humidity was terrible. We crossed a small river and were so thirsty we filled our canteens directly from the river and drank heartily, then filled them up again before getting to the other side. When we got about half a mile past the river, it doubled back, and we had to cross it again. This was upstream from where we had crossed before.

As we neared the river, I saw something that made me want to throw up. There were several bodies of North Vietnamese soldiers that had rotted in the river. There were also water buffalo they had been using to carry supplies. They apparently had been blown away by an airstrike. The water buffalo and the men floating in the water were bloated and full of maggots. And that water was flowing around those bodies and downstream to where we had been when we drank the water and filled up our canteens. We dumped our canteens and refilled them farther upstream, but the damage had already been done.

There was something else we encountered on this operation. A liquid was dripping all over us and soaked through our clothes. It was on the ground, in the trees, everywhere. We later learned it was Agent Orange, which had been sprayed to kill all of the vegetation, and we were in the thick of it. Many guys got cancer later in life from that spraying. I just know it is still inside of me, just waiting to attack. I still cannot believe that the Marine Corps knowingly sent us into that area after it was so saturated with Agent Orange, also called dioxin. It had been banned in the United States for years because of its cancer-causing agents. Another war-machine profit in the United States by Dow Chemical. I hope your stock went up enough during the war to satisfy your full pockets with Johnson money.

We marched all day until eventually getting close to where the ambush had been. We lost some guys to booby traps in the area, but thankfully, we received no gunfire. All of a sudden, a figure ran out of the jungle, screaming at the top of his lungs, "They are everywhere, run and hide! They will kill you all!"

He was ragged, dirty, dehydrated, and literally out of his mind. During the next few minutes, five others exited the jungle in the same manner. We almost shot each one of them when they came running out. None of them had a weapon or gear. One was coherent enough to tell us they had been hiding from the North Vietnamese without food or water for the last three or four days. We fed them and gave them water. He then said the rear squad of the two platoon patrol had been ambushed by twin .50-caliber machine guns the

North Vietnamese had positioned in a cross fire just up the trail. They had been just ahead of the ambush, and they thought the first platoon had been totally wiped out, leaving only them alive. The others kept screaming to get them out of there because the "gooks" were everywhere.

We got them back to the rear of our company and proceeded forward. I was told to take the point, and when I rounded the next trail, I held up my hand for the rest of the company to halt. What I saw still haunts me to this day. The entire squad was on the ground, each man with about fifty bullet holes in him. They had been lying in the 120-degree heat for over four days, and their bodies had started to bloat. They were full of worms and maggots.

I will never forget two of the marines. The picture is in my head every day. One had apparently hit the ground when the fire started from the ambush. He was prone on the ground with his rife pointed toward the jungle, and his finger was on the trigger with the safety off. His buddy was lying on top of him, as if to protect him from the hail of bullets pelting their bodies. It was a picture I wish I would have taken so it could have been published in every newspaper in the United States to show what we were doing over there, the sacrifices being made, the lives being lost, the courage being exhibited every minute of every day, and the love one human being can have for another one, even to give up his life to try to save another person.

This is the picture I have in my mind every day, and I hope those reading this book will now reflect on this, appreciate what we did over there, and also understand why we should have never been there. In all, there were about thirteen dead marines in a straight line going up a small hill. My camera was back at base camp in my seabag I never saw again.

I called Sergeant Wenger, and he immediately deployed several of us ahead to set up a secure area in case we were running into an ambush. After several minutes, we heard two explosions. We took cover, thinking we were being mortared, then I heard Sergeant Wenger yell out, "Stop the body bagging, they are booby-trapped!"

We lost four marines that day, as they lifted the bodies of two of the dead squad members to put them into body bags. The booby traps were pressure sensitive. When the bodies were lifted off the pins, explosions took the four marines while injuring several others nearby with shrapnel. The North Vietnamese had planted these booby traps knowing we would take our dead out and they add to the body count this way.

We were called back to assist with the body removal because I was carrying a hundred-foot rope. We started tying the rope to a foot of each marine, taking care not to move the bodies off the pressure sensors. We made sure everyone was clear, then we removed the dog tags of each marine so whatever we had left in parts could be sent home to the families of each man. We were in shock when we saw what little was left to send home after we jerked the bodies off the booby traps. I thought of the families forced to have a closed-casket funeral, but at least they would be able to know something left of their marine would be in the casket. My mind strayed back to Mike Allen. We found an arm and a leg, and that was all we sent home. The rest of his body had been all over me and had to be picked and washed off. I was slipping into a depressed state. Sergeant Wenger snapped all of us back to the present with a shout to get our war faces back on.

We cleared the area with detonation cord wrapped around enough trees to create a landing zone in the middle of the jungle and called in the choppers to take the bodies away. The North Vietnamese were skilled in psychological warfare; this day had affected all of us negatively. We loaded our dead onto choppers and moved north.

THE ROCK PILE

At our last reunion of G-2/7, several of us were given a lapel pin. It was a resemblance of the Rock Pile, a huge mountain we lived at for several weeks. We would run operations and patrols off it and set up ambushes. It was a strategic area, close to the Ho Chi Minh trail, in the DMZ. This area was bombed constantly by B52s because of the men and equipment the North Vietnamese were running down the trail into South Vietnam. We were constantly sniped at and mortared occasionally, but overall, for being so far north, it wasn't too bad. We dug foxholes down into the ground to protect us from the blasts of direct hits and shrapnel. We were told it would work, but I never knew anyone who took a direct hit and survived. We dug them anyway.

The worst thing was getting resupplied. The helicopters would start to come in to resupply us, and they would get shot down by the enemy. We were a full day's march from Dong Ha, and supplies were getting dangerously low. We were running out of food and water, and the North Vietnamese knew it. We had enough firepower with us. They really didn't want a confrontation, but they could sure mess with us by shooting down any choppers that came.

If that wasn't enough, the entire platoon was struck with dysentery. I don't know what caused it, but everyone got it, and it was really bad. We would go to the bathroom, and then five minutes later, we would have to go again. Doc McKeen ran out of pills, and it got worse. We ran out of places to go to the bathroom and actually started going in our foxholes, hoping we didn't need to take cover in them. We were all miserably tired, hungry, and dehydrated. I think Sergeant Wenger knew we were all at our limit. He finally ordered us back to Dong Ha the next morning for medical attention and supplies.

That night, we looked up to our right and saw an entire company of North Vietnamese with lanterns headed away from us. They knew they were out of rifle range. I think it was their way of rubbing it in our faces. We were in luck, though. They had never heard about Puff the Magic Dragon. It was finally payback time for what they had done to our marines. Puff the Magic Dragon was an air force plane that was full of Gatling guns. One burst of those guns would put a 7.62MM round in every square foot of a football field.

We called in an airstrike on the North Vietnamese company and waited. We heard the sound of a plane, and then we saw the bright light come down from the sky like a huge lightning bolt, followed by the unmistakable *buuuuuurrrrrppp*! of Puff firing all of its guns at the same time at the target. The lanterns were extinguished instantly, with a company of dead North Vietnamese.

We saddled up the next morning for the long march back to Dong Ha, with all of us having to stop beside the trail many, many times to use the bathroom. We arrived back at Dong Ha and received a not-so-warm welcome. We had not had a bath, changed clothes, brushed teeth, or shaved for two weeks, during which we had diarrhea. We were tired, hungry, and not in a mood for any crap from the air force. We started to go through the chow line to get a hot meal. They acted like we had some type of deadly highly contagious disease. They did not want us eating their food with their utensils or their mess gear. They refused to let us use anything.

Sergeant Wenger had a good solution: take out the helmet liner and use it for holding food. We went through the mess line, and they piled everything they had into our helmets on top of each food item. We didn't care and started eating with our fingers, food dropping from our mouths while the air force cooks looked on in total disgust. We growled at them, and they all left the mess hall to us. We ate our fill and then started a food fight. It had been a while since we had just played around, and it relieved much of the tension we carried back from the jungle.

We showered, got medications, and resupplied with ammo. The air force said they didn't have enough C rations for us, and we would have to wait until we were resupplied. Sergeant Wenger received orders telling us to go back to the Rock Pile as soon as we were able to move out. He selected several of us to go on a midnight raid of the supply depot of the air force. We went to the fenced-in area of their supply depot and made a cradle out of our hands to help each other over the fence. We then very stealthily cut through one of the tents with our bayonets and stole about forty cases of C rations. We had an assembly line going to throw the cases over the fence. We also stole several canisters of water.

We made it back to the company and our squad. We distributed the food, giving each guy about three days' worth of food and a full canteen. When we got back to the staging area, we all had a good hot meal. We were fortunate that night, not having to stand guard duty and getting a little extra sleep. I know that doesn't sound like such a big deal, but in Vietnam, a full night's sleep was really big.

At about 5:00 a.m., the base got hit by some type of artillery, which we later found out was a recoilless rifle being fired from within the vicinity of the Rock Pile. They made a direct hit on several ammo dumps, resulting in the death of several of the air force guys. Thankfully, we were far enough away to be out of range.

BACK TO THE ROCK PILE

After a one-day delay from the recoilless rifles wreaking havoc on the base and our troops, we set out to return to the Rock Pile. Our job now was to go back in with three companies and take out the recoilless rifles. What we didn't know was we were going to be bait used to discover where a division of the NVA was so our guys could send in B52s for an airstrike. The base didn't know they would get hit that soon by the rifles, and they lost many men because of that blunder.

We left early the morning after the attack and were glad to get away from the base. It seemed the base was a sitting duck for future attacks with no defense. We made it to the Rock Pile with only one attack from a wood line, and we took out many Vietnamese, but they were not the hard troops we were looking for. I never knew if Sergeant Wenger knew we were being bait or not, but if he did, he never told us.

The following morning, we were successfully resupplied by choppers that weren't shot down. We got in a new lieutenant, and everyone was furious. There we were, going into a bad situation that would probably include a huge battle, and we had a newbie leading us instead of Sergeant Wenger. The new lieutenant looked like he was younger than us, and he was cocky. We dug in on the Rock Pile again and started running patrols off the pile.

The next night, we heard "Incoming!" and we all jumped into our holes. We had a perimeter set up around the Rock Pile, and we were pretty high up, but we were sitting ducks. Any NVA could easily sneak up on us in the dark and slit our throats. We were already keyed up and terrified. Visions of what they had done to E (Echo) 2/4 were still in our minds.

I heard the first whine of a mortar go over our heads. I knew we were in for it. The funny thing about hearing the whine of the mortar is that it scares the crap out of you, but if you hear the whine, it means it has already safely passed you by. But you cannot tell that to your protective mind, so you hit the ground anyway. Graham and I jumped into our foxhole. It was starting to be the worst night of my life.

They threw everything they had at us. The rounds were exploding so close to our foxhole, but we were actually getting thrown around in the hole by the explosions. It was so loud we lost our hearing. We thought it was probably an assault, and we should be standing in our hole to protect ourselves against the attack, but we were so scared of the constant explosions above us we couldn't move. We started counting. At some point, the number reached 110 explosions. I have no idea how we would have survived a direct hit coming into our hole, but luckily, that didn't happen.

I remember talking to Graham about his life and his thoughts that God didn't exist. He had told me before he was an atheist. When we were in the hole getting bounced around and with mortars hitting all around us, my life seemed as though it could be over any second with a direct hit. I tried to talk to Graham about faith, God, and his soul. I felt that night he accepted Christ and actually started believing in a supreme being that could guide his life. I hope he did.

The mortars continued all through the night. When it became light in the morning, the mortars stopped. Graham started to stand up. I tried to pull him down, but he peeked over the top of the hole to see what it looked like around our hole. Another mortar hit right at that moment, and he fell back into the hole, grabbing at his forehead. Blood was streaming from his head. I got out a bandage and applied it to his head, immediately applying pressure. I called for Doc McKeen, and we got Graham evacuated on the next chopper. You should know it wasn't that bad of an injury, he had just caught a small piece of shrapnel. He was back in two days after they stitched him up.

After Graham was evacuated, I got a call to go to Sergeant Wenger's hole. As I walked up to his hole about fifty feet away, rounds started flying all around me. A sniper had me zeroed in. Every time I changed direction, another round was whizzing by my head or hitting at the ground around me. Everyone was jumping into their holes and crying out. There must have been several snipers because many guys were hit, one dead. I jumped into the first hole I saw, and rounds continued hitting all around the hole I jumped into. The fire stopped, and we cautiously peeked out of our holes, only to have it start again. Back into the hole I went. There were two guys in the hole and it was crowded, but it protected us. We stayed there for about twenty minutes until no further rounds were coming in. I got out and headed for Sergeant Wenger's hole.

He started the conversation by saying we had lost two guys to the mortars, and we were lucky. He said we were going to send out a two-squad patrol to see if we encountered anything, and he wanted me to be point. I usually ran a double point with Graham, so another marine, my friend Cecil Covel, was selected for my second point man.

We were on very high alert, moving cautiously through the jungle. There was a small trail there. I couldn't believe we were told to follow the trail. It was probably loaded with booby traps and mines. Cecil and I were careful with every step. All of a sudden, there appeared across the trial the biggest snake I have ever seen. It was at least a foot wide. I didn't see its head; I just saw ten feet of it stretched across the trail, moving swiftly. Another five feet went by as I stood there in shock. Cecil came up to where I stood. He could not believe what he was seeing.

Sergeant Wenger and the other guys in the rear were getting antsy. "What is the hold up?"

I sent back the word, "Big snake!"

The word came back. "What kind of snake?"

I sent back the word, "Big f——ing snake!"

We stopped until all thirty feet of it passed by. I don't know what kind of a snake it was, but the only thing

I can think of is some kind of giant python. When it cleared the trail, we started moving again.

I came across some North Vietnamese communication wire stretched across the trail. I knew it was North Vietnamese because it was white, and ours was black. I sent back word to Sergeant Wenger I had found com wire across the trail and awaited his order.

"Cut it, and fall back!" was the reply.

I did what I was told, and Cecil and I fell back.

We went back to the rest of the platoon and became rear security. We made it back to the Rock Pile and settled in for the night. We had not been resupplied for several days. Every helicopter that tried to land in our landing zone was shot at so many times they refused to bring us any supplies. We had not eaten for two days. Several of us were sitting together on the top of a hill on the Rock Pile, talking. We were talking about God and Vietnam. Some of the guys said they had a really bad feeling about tomorrow.

I remember Bob Pabst, Cecil Covel, Corporal Minor, and Graham being there. It was a beautiful night; there were no mortars, no snipers, and it was incredibly peaceful. I kept telling one guy not to be concerned, and he kept telling me he knew he was going to get it tomorrow. We made fun of him a little to get him to relax. Little did we know he would be one of those killed the next day.

We heard a chopper approaching and dove to the holes right away because we knew sniper fire would be coming in for the chopper. We were looking forward to food and water. Then we noticed something was wrong when the chopper didn't have time to hover and drop off supplies. It just came in and left. We figured he had received sniper fire and took off before dropping supplies.

Shortly after we came out of our holes, I got a call to come to the CP. I went to the CP, and they gave me an envelope from the Red Cross. I took it back to the guys and opened it, reading by the flame of a lighter. The letter said, "Mom and son doing well, 8 pounds 10 ounces."

I was elated. I was the father of a healthy baby boy. His name was Chris, as Barb and I had decided when I was home getting married. All the guys congratulated me. The guys in my squad had put money in a hat guessing how much my baby would weigh when it was born, so we checked to see who had come closest to the weight. I won. I collected sixty dollars from everyone. To this day, I am thankful to the pilot who risked his life to bring me the news of my son's birth. I was thrilled and also depressed at the same time. I thought then more than ever, will I make it home to see my family again?

I remember sitting there that night under a full moon with Cecil Covel, Bob Papst, Jim Graham, Lopez, Corporal Minor, and Bob Montgomery. We were all hungry, thirsty, and tired, and more than anything, we were scared. This was the worst combat we had seen, it was the closest we had been to an enemy force, and we didn't know where they were, but in with all the darkness, it was a great night to share the birth of my son. I had the support of all my brothers with me that night. The brotherhood developed is something I cannot explain.

It goes beyond the love and closeness of brothers, and it can only be understood by those who were together 24-7 for many months enduring hardships, death, and pain, all at the same time watching out for each other and sharing with each other in a common bond.

The next morning, there was still no resupply. I got called to Sergeant Wenger's foxhole, and he said we were going out on a two-company patrol with Graham and me on point. I asked Sergeant Wenger where we were going. We were looking for a recoilless rifle battery in possession of the North Vietnamese at that point. Our job was to search them out and destroy them because they were still firing on the base at Dong Ha.

I asked Sergeant Wenger which direction to go and what the plans were for the patrol. He said we were going out on the same trail we had been on yesterday, where we found the com wire.

I said to him bluntly, "No disrespect, sir, but you have to be s——ing me!"

His response was, "No. I am not. The new lieutenant is in charge, and those are his orders."

I told Sergeant Wenger I felt the new lieutenant was going to get us all killed.

"Just do what you're told."

We got ready, being sure to pack extra ammo and grenades. Then we started out. I didn't run into any booby traps, but I was treading extremely cautiously. I didn't want to run into Mr. Snake again. I just knew he was waiting for me, hiding in the jungle, waiting to wrap around me and choke the life from me. I hate snakes.

Graham was directly behind me when we suddenly came up on the white com wire we had cut the day before. We both saw it at the same time, and our blood curdled. The wire had been spliced back together. This was not good, ten thousand miles from home. I knew I was going to die that day. I held up a hand in the air to halt. The word came back up to me: "What is the hold up?"

I sent word back about the spliced wire we had cut the day before. The word was passed back to me to "cut it and follow it."

I hesitated, questioning the order. Word came back to us, the order repeated. We did as we were told. I checked my rifle and put it in a jungle sling so I could shoot from the hip. I had it on full automatic, I flipped the trigger guard to fire instead of the usual safe, and I unsnapped the magazine pouches on my web belt. We were travelling slowly up a slight grade since we left and were approaching the top of the hill. The jungle was thick on each side of the five-foot-wide trail. I saw sudden movement in front of me, and I knew right away Graham had seen it too because he moved up beside me instead of being about five feet behind.

We were almost to the top of the hill when six soldiers appeared on the same trail in front of me. I was shocked, they were shocked. We just stood there and stared at each other for what seemed to be an eternity, but I know now it was only seconds. I remember seeing four North Vietnamese and two Red Chinese. I remember wondering, *What are Red Chinese doing here?* I knew they were Red Chinese because they were bigger, and the red star was on their covers. None of them were wearing helmets. I knew they were NVA right away because they were in full brown uniform.

While we were staring at each other, I saw each soldier had an AK47, but they did not have them up. They didn't know we were there, just like we didn't know they were there. Except we were prepared for a confrontation after finding the com wire reconnected.

I had my M14 ready to rock and roll with my finger on the trigger, and that is the only thing that saved me. My rife was up and theirs were down. Graham and I started firing and saw them go down; it was hard to miss with only twenty feet in between us. What we didn't know was on the other side of the hill was a full regiment of NVA. We heard later there were about 1,200 of them, and I had walked right into their camp as they were sending out a patrol just like we were.

After we emptied our magazines, all hell broke loose. Rounds started flying everywhere. Graham and I took cover behind a large fallen tree and lay down. Bullets flew all over, hitting the tree right above our heads. I didn't know what the hell we had gotten into, so Graham and I pulled back to Sergeant Wenger to report. He demanded to know what was going on. I told him we had run into a patrol, and we had shot the six we saw. Then more rounds started flying right above our heads. They knew we were there, but they didn't know exactly where.

The fire was so intense, and there was nowhere to hide, so we all just instinctively hit the ground. We had no visible enemy to shoot at through the thickness of the jungle. Graham was beside me when we got separated from the rest of the platoon. Everyone was just trying to avoid being shot by the hail of fire. We couldn't see through the trees, so we just started firing in the general direction of where the bullets were coming from. This was a mistake; this is what they were waiting for. The rate of incoming fire increased all around Graham and me.

The only cover I could find was a small tree in front of me. I put my helmet to the ground, and I know hundreds of rounds went right above my head. When I finally looked up to search for targets to shoot at, I looked at the tree I hid behind, and the tree was gone. There had been such intense fire coming at me it had disintegrated the tree. It wasn't there anymore. I spared a look at Graham. We both wore the same expression of absolute terror.

I told him we needed to pull back, and then it started. *Whomp*! *Whomp*! They had zeroed in on us and were launching mortars at us. Explosions were going off everywhere. It was deafening. If someone would have tried to speak to me, I wouldn't have heard them. We started to pull back to where we thought Sergeant Wenger was, but we ran across a wounded marine lying along the side of the trail instead. I slung my weapon and bent over to pick him up to pull him back to safety. Then everything happened in slow motion.

A mortar hit right behind me. It blew me into the air. I lost my weapon and hit the ground face-first. I was in shock. I know, because I knew I been hit, but there was no pain. I felt blood running from every part of my body. I could not breathe. I would find out later a piece of shrapnel had gone through my chest, into my right lung, and it had deflated. I could not move my right arm, it was dead. I finally got to my senses enough to realize I was bleeding profusely from an artery in my neck. I knew I was going to die. Everything flashed through my mind at once. I will not see my parents again, or my family or friends. I will never see Barb again. I will never see my son grow up.

I was ten thousand miles from home, and no one would know what happened to me. I remember very little from that point on, but I do remember a few things. I remember lying on the ground and knowing I was dying. Then something said to me, "Put your finger into the hole in your neck." I know now it was God saving my life. I took my finger and found the hole in my neck the blood was squirting out of every time my heart beat. I put my index finger from my left hand into the hole to the second digit, and the blood flow stopped. I had been hit in my carotid artery, and my brachial plexus had been severed, which was why my right arm went dead. I was gasping for air with every breath. Interestingly enough, I still felt no pain at this point. I was still in shock. The pain would come later.

The first thing I remember after that is being with three other guys. I don't know who they were, but none of us could shoot a gun. None of us had any weapon of any kind. I remember us hiding in some brush along the trail as we heard several North Vietnamese voices close to where we were. They were looking for us. I am sure they would have killed us or imprisoned us. We remained hidden from the ten or so NVA. I have never been so scared. For some reason, they went a different direction, and we didn't see them again.

We then moved out and tried to find anyone who could help us. I remember one of the guys I was with had been shot in the butt several times. I still don't know how he was walking, but then I don't know how I was still conscious either. Miraculously we somehow managed to get back to where Sergeant Wenger was. I collapsed on the ground. Rounds were flying, and mortars were going off all around us.

I remember Sergeant Wenger standing there like a rock, telling men what to do—no fear, just plain hard guts. I remember him getting Doc McKeen to see what he could do for me. I remember Doc coming over and looking at me. He turned to Sergeant Wenger and said, "There is nothing I can do for him, he's gone." I could not speak because my lung was collapsed, and breathing was a chore, much less trying to speak. I wanted to tell Doc, "Fix me up and make me stop bleeding," but nothing came out. At our reunion forty years later, Bob Pabst told me I had kept saying in a shocked child's voice, "Does anyone know first aid, and can you stop this bleeding?"

I think I remember two machine gun teams being told by Sergeant Wenger to go forward and try to set up a defensive fire. I learned later neither team had made it very far before they were hit by heavy fire. I was also told Doc McKeen went forward to try to save some of them. He was shot several times before he died; he was trying to do his best to save as many as he could. Unfortunately, his efforts were in vain. All eight of the machine gun team members died that day, and Doc as well. Doc was later awarded the Navy Cross for his heroism. I will never forget him.

I remember lying there on the ground with no weapon, waiting for the NVA to overrun us at any second. I looked up to the sky and silently said to God, "I am ready to go, just take me." The pain started to sink in, and it was unbearable. But for some reason, God didn't want me that day. I also remember thinking, *If you get me through this, I will do whatever you want me to do.* Later in my life, God led me to teach Sunday school, and I have for the last forty-five years, teaching junior and senior high kids at the churches I have been at over the years. Every Sunday, for forty-five years before class and before going in to work, I've said this prayer: "Give me the words to say, I am your voice, not that my will be done but yours."

Please don't think for a moment I am a saint. I am not. And I have done many things wrong in my life, more than I care to admit. I have tried to live a good life but have fallen short on many occasions, as my wife can testify to, but I remember the promise I made to God that day in Vietnam to do whatever he wanted me to do. I can only hope I have been a mentor to many kids in my classes, changing at least a few of their lives, and if this is a fact, I have fulfilled my promise. I have survived ten holes in me from mortars many times in Vietnam where I should have died, a brain tumor, a stroke, and ten years on the highway patrol. God had a plan for my life, and he still does. I am still teaching

Sunday school every Sunday and have the full support of my wife in this venture, even at sixty-six years old.

I remember after making this promise to God something told me to get up and start moving. I remember getting with several other wounded guys. One guy had a radio, and we called in for a medevac chopper to pick us up. I remember them directing us to come to a clearing about a hundred yards away from the action so they could pick us up. I had no idea where we were going; I just stumbled along with the rest of the guys. Along the trail on our way to the chopper pickup, I saw many dead and wounded.

I never saw Sergeant Wenger again and later learned from Cecil they had made an assault on the hill and caught the NVA out in the open. They had killed many that day. He told of one North Vietnamese who started running down the hill, screaming and firing at him and Sergeant Wenger. Cecil said he took his BAR, a heavy-duty automatic M14, and emptied it into the guy to finally get him to stop. He said he will never forget that moment. Cecil was hit but not seriously wounded.

Along the trail to the chopper, I saw something that has haunted me every night for the past forty-eight years. Corporal Minor was sitting beside a tree on the trail. It looked like he had just stopped for a rest. The only problem was he had a hole in the center of his head, and he had totally bled out. He was as white as snow. There was blood all around him, and he was just staring straight ahead.

The next thing I remember is arriving in the clearing where the chopper picked us up. I looked down as the chopper lifted off, and a mortar hit exactly where the chopper had been sitting. The machine gunner was firing nonstop at targets on the ground. We flew for a long while until we arrived at Dong Ha, where we were put into a room in wheelchairs. There were so many casualties they couldn't handle them. I must have passed out after sitting around with some of the guys that were hit. I remember Lopez being there, but that is all. The next thing I remember is waking up in a hospital ward in Da Nang. I was in a hospital bed, with battle dressings all over me. I felt my neck for the hole I had used my finger to plug before, and I had wire stitches.

A corpsman told me I had been in surgery and was going to be okay. They had repaired my brachial plexus the best that they could, and they had taken out several pieces of shrapnel. The doctor who operated on me said he had asked me before he started surgery if I wanted him to take out all of the shrapnel since it was really deep and the surgery would be extensive. He said he could just leave it in, and he thought it would be all right. I opted not to have the shrapnel removed. I don't remember any of this conversation. He said he had operated on my neck. About 60% of the nerves in my brachial plexus had been torn apart and he had done his best to put them back together. Hopefully with time, they would reconnect themselves.

I was in the hospital in Da Nang for about three weeks. While I was there, I was told General Walt would be around one morning to give me my second Purple Heart. I became very woozy, and I kept asking the corpsman to check my dressings because I thought I was bleeding. They ignored this, and I finally passed out. I eventually woke to a corpsman slapping my face. They had waited too long to check on me. My wounds had opened up, and the bed was totally covered in my blood. The general was about to arrive, and they didn't have enough time to change the sheets. I remember them begging me not to say anything to the general as they covered me up with fresh linens. Underneath I was a bloody mess. The general came with his staff and pinned my second Purple Heart on my pillow. They took a picture with a Polaroid camera and gave it to me. I cannot even remember what the general said to me because I was ready to pass out again from losing so much blood. I still have that photo in my office at my home today.

Many people will not like what I am about to say about the Red Cross, but I was in the hospital, and my family had not heard from me. I could not write a letter home because my right arm was still dead, and I had nothing to write with. There was a Red Cross person on our ward every day. You would think this was a good thing for the troops lying in bed, eyes shot out, burnt, missing limbs, and depressed and lonely. You would think on our ward of about a hundred marines the Red Cross person would have his hands full with writing letters for them, comforting them, getting them something to drink, and generally caring for them.

This was not the case. In the person's mind, his job was to attend the doctors' meetings at the end of the ward every morning and take them coffee and doughnuts. This was not all bad in itself, but he would push his cart of fresh coffee and doughnuts past the wounded guys, and when they would ask him for a doughnut or a cup of coffee, he would just keep going without even responding to them. He would flat out ignore all of us. He would then take the coffee and doughnuts to the officers, and they would have a good ole time in front of all of us. I never saw him help any of the troops, and we all despised him.

I stopped the Red Cross person one morning, concerned about my family and what they were thinking because I had not been able to send them a letter to let them know I was okay. I asked him to write a letter home for me since I couldn't write. He said he didn't have time for that and just kept walking. A corpsman standing nearby heard the conversation, called the Red Cross person an asshole to his face, and proceeded to sit down and write the letter for me. It made the weeks at the hospital in Da Nang more bearable, and then I was told I would be transferred to a hospital in the Philippines.

THE PHILIPPINES AND JAPAN

We were put on stretchers and loaded onto ambulances that took us to a medevac C-130. We flew to the Philippines via Vietnam, where we stopped and took on more wounded marines. It was frightening to think how many choppers had been shot down doing what we were doing, landing to take on the wounded. Thankfully it went without incident, and we were only on the ground for about thirty minutes.

When we reached the Philippines, we went directly to a hospital ward. I was there for five where I was treated very well. I know it sounds crazy, but I became very afraid, worse than I had been in Vietnam. I was around people that looked the same as the people I had been killing. It was the first time I realized I did not have my M14 in my hands. I felt naked and vulnerable. Despite the good treatment, those five days were like living a bad dream.

After the days spent in the Philippines, we were put onto a plane to Japan. There was one other marine with me, and his name was Bob Kole. Bob and I became good friends. Bob had been shot in the head on a force recon mission. He had a sunken part of his head that was scary to look at. The bullet that hit him had shattered his skull and affected his speech and thought process. He was depressed, so every day I tried to lift his spirits.

Little did I know our records had been sent to a naval hospital in Yachuska, Japan, where we were supposed to go. By mistake, we were sent to the 106th General Hospital in Yokohoma, Japan, which was an all-army hospital. My apprehension at being around all-army airborne troops soon came to an end when the guys on our ward welcomed us with open arms. We were not allowed to leave the base or even go off the ward until we were checked out by a surgeon. I remember the doctor well. His name was Dr. Pearson, and he was a cool guy. He was independently wealthy and had his Corvette shipped to him for his tour in Japan.

I remember when Dr. Pearson first met with me; he asked me if I knew where my medical records were. I was shocked and told him I had no idea. He asked me what happened to me, and I told him. He was surprised I was alive. He checked my right arm, and I could hardly move it. He said it was a miracle the doctor in Vietnam had put the nerves from the biracial plexus together, and I was lucky they didn't have to amputate my arm. He thought some physical therapy could help my arm, and he would put me on a breathing machine every day to build back up the breathing capability of my right lung.

I thought it was crazy, but his idea of physical therapy was shooting a bow and arrow every day. I actually got pretty good with the bow, and I felt the strength coming back to my arm. I remember Dr.

Pearson telling me I would suffer greatly in about twenty years because the damaged nerves in my right arm would start to deteriorate and cause pain. I had no idea what he meant at that time, but twenty years later, the pain came with a vengeance, and I am still suffering every day.

The real experience for the six weeks I was in Yokohoma was every morning looking off the balcony of the fourteenth floor of the hospital and seeing the sun rise over Mt. Fuji. It was breathtaking. The other experience was meeting all the unique characters on my ward. There were guys with burns so bad their entire bodies were covered in bandages, and they would scream in pain every day. There were amputees whom I would sit and talk to and cry with about the future of their lives and how fate had dealt them such a terrible blow.

I remember one sergeant on our ward who was totally insane. He had done three tours in Vietnam and had been hit and was recuperating, but his biggest problem wasn't physical, it was mental. He would not talk with anyone. I would say hi to him, and he would just keep walking. Every day he would go to the PX (post-exchange store) and buy a model airplane or tank. He would come back to his bed and spend the day meticulously putting them together and painting them in detail. They were beautiful. When he finished with the model, he would go to the window of the fourteenth floor, open it, and, with a smile on his face, throw the model out the window to watch it crash into the pavement. He would laugh very loudly and then immediately head back to the PX to buy more models he could put together and throw out the window.

I was issued an army uniform with no insignias on it, and I was told Kole and me were the only marines at the hospital. The army guys treated us as brothers. When we were finally allowed to go on liberty, they took me with them even though I had no money. My records had not caught up to me, so I couldn't get paid. They took me to a bar in Yokohoma, where I was first introduced to sake. I remember having a few of them and looking around the bar, thinking I was dreaming. I saw my friend and trainer Mike Allen, who had been killed in Vietnam. I sat there and probably turned white. There he stood with several of his friends at the bar. I could not stand it any longer, so I walked over to him and asked him what his name was.

Jim Allen.

I asked him if he had a brother named Mike.

He said, "Yes, did you know him?"

I said I had been with him when he died, and immediately he started crying. He then told me he was Mike's twin. He said his family had received a casket that was closed and was told not to open it. They didn't know what had happened. It was as though God had sent me to him to give him some much-needed closure about Mike's death.

He asked me to sit with him alone, and we talked for several hours about Mike. What kind of a person he was, how he had trained me and stuck with me when all of the other guys in the squad had turned their backs on me because I was a new guy. I told him about how

Mike was killed, and that we only found an arm and a leg and the rest of him was grafted onto me. We cried, hugged, and prayed. I finally left him and told the guys I was with that I needed to go back to the hospital. One of the guys rode with me in a taxi to make sure I got back to the base. I was not myself for several days.

I had not been at the hospital in Japan long when they did a blood test on me and I was tested for hookworm. They told me I had the worst case they had ever seen and proceeded to give me a double dose of the hookworm treatment, which meant swallowing pure alcohol pills. It was supposed to kill the hookworm immediately, but it made me so drunk I was not allowed to get out of my bed for twenty-four hours. I thought back to when I probably got the hookworm, remembering the dead NVA and water buffalo floating in the river we crossed and drank from.

While in Japan, Kole had major surgery, and they put a plate in his head so he would actually appear normal. I continued my therapy for the remainder of my time in Japan and went out on liberty several times with my army buddies. They would pay for my drinks whenever we went to bars, and they would up pick up prostitutes. I would just sit and wait on them and pray they didn't get some type of disease from the girls. I never did anything like that because I stayed true to Barb the entire time I was away from her, and she did the same.

Finally I was told I would be headed back to the States, and it was approaching Christmas. I sent a letter to Barb and told her I was coming home. I also told my parents. We were put on stretchers and put on a medevac flight from Japan to Alaska. We arrived in Alaska, and it was 30 degrees below zero. We rushed from the plane to the building off the runway. I have never been so cold in all my life. They fed us, and then back on the plane we went, headed for Washington, DC on Christmas Eve.

We arrived in DC, and it was very empty where they sent us. I still don't know where we were. The amazing thing was we were treated very well by corpsmen there. The best thing was after being depressed so long, we were finally home on Christmas Eve. But we were alone. There were three elderly women from some local organization who came into our ward with milk and cookies for us. They sat with us and sang Christmas songs. I will never forget these women who instead of being with their families on Christmas Eve came to the hospital to spend time with some marines they didn't even know. They also paid for one phone call home for each of us. I called Barb and was allowed to speak with her for five minutes. I wished her a merry Christmas, ate my cookies, and went to bed.

ARRIVING HOME

After being checked out by a doctor in DC, we were told we would be given a week of liberty to go home to see our families. I was issued new uniforms and my ribbons and medals. I was now an E3, or lance corporal, having been promoted in Vietnam. I cannot remember how I got the ticket to get home, but I flew. I called Barb and told her I would be flying from DC to Dayton, and gave her my arrival time. I was finally going home. I shined my shoes and made sure my uniform was looking good, and I was squared away. I could not wait to see my family and Barb, and my son for the first time.

What I didn't know was what Barb had done. It made the first time I saw my son and Barb very special. She told my family she did not want them to come to the airport, that this was a time for her and Chris and me. And what a time it was. I got off the plane and got my luggage. Then I saw them, Barb holding Chris with her back to me. I walked up to her and tapped her on the shoulder. She turned around. She looked fantastic, as she always does. She had her winter coat on, Chris was all bundled up, and she smelled so good. She was beautiful then, and still is now.

I reached out, and we hugged and kissed for I don't know how long. The rest of the airport disappeared, and we were by ourselves in our own world, loving each other, holding Chris and just staring at each other and our son. This was one of the best moments of my life. A very personable time between us and family would come later. Barb's mother wasn't even there. We stayed at the airport for a long time, just enjoying the moment. I cannot remember what we said to each other, and it really doesn't matter. It was a moment in time just for us to be together, to love each other, and to see my son for the first time. He was about four months old when I first saw him and held him. When I held him, I thought about Graham, Minor, Doc McKeen, Bob Montgomery, and all the other guys killed that fateful day who would never have the chance to have a moment like this.

After a night at Barb's mom's apartment, the next day was spent seeing family, having dinner, and telling stories. The biggest problem I had with the stories was in the Marine Corps, you cuss often; it is just expected. While sitting around with the family at my parents' house, the big f-word came out, and I saw the shocked look on my parents' faces. It was not good.

Uncle Carl, who was in the army in World War II, saved me. He broke the silence and reiterated what I said without the f-word. He then asked another question, and we moved on to another subject. The week went by too quickly, and then I had to head back to the hospital I had been assigned to for recuperation, the Philadelphia Naval Hospital in Pennsylvania. I remember when I was home, it seemed as though everyone was different. I finally realized it was not other people who were different: it was me, and I would never be the same again. What I had seen and done had changed me forever.

THE HOSPITAL FROM HELL

I arrived in Philadelphia and checked into the hospital. The reception was not as I had expected. The people who checked us in were cold, abusive, and completely unsympathetic to us. We did not expect a hero's welcome, but we at least expected to be treated as human beings. This was not to happen. This would prove to be one of the worst parts of my life. The hospital was old and dirty. The doctors were few, and they did nothing for me while I was there, except harass me.

There was a chief in the navy there who was in charge of work details for all of the patients. I could not believe it when I was there for just a few days and saw this chief screaming at all of the wounded marines. He belittled everyone and threatened them with demotion if they didn't do exactly what he said. I actually saw him assign work details such as emptying cigarette butt containers on the wards and in the hallways to single amputees. They would go through and empty the ashtrays. When the chief came around for one of his three daily inspections, if there was a cigarette in an ashtray, he would write up the amputee for failure to follow his orders. The bad thing about this situation was if the amputee or any of the wounded guys got demoted, their disability checks would be less because the checks were based on your rank.

Fed up with this treatment, I went to him and told him what I thought about the situation. He threatened to write me up too if I opened my mouth again. I tried going to a doctor on our ward but was told to mind my own business. The doctors there were no better than the chief. It was just like the Red Cross person in Vietnam.

No one visited the amputee ward. All they had was the guys on the ward who were ambulatory to help the others. I remember one guy with his face burned so badly he looked like a monster. On the ward, he would not wear the mask they had given him because his face was so hideous. He was married, and I vividly recall the first time his young wife came to the ward unexpectedly to see him. She saw him without his mask. She looked at him, covered her mouth in disgust, and fled the hospital without speaking to him. He was devastated, saying he didn't want to live any longer. We stayed up all night talking to him, making sure he didn't try to kill himself. The next day, he received divorce papers from his wife, and he cried for days.

I was walking through one of the amputee wards one day, and to my astonishment, I saw one of the guys who were with me when I got hit. He had lost both legs and one arm. I was stunned. I had to pull myself together to even speak to him. The last thing he needed was me stammering over the sight of him like that. I sat and talked with him for a long time, and we went over what each of us remembered about getting hit that day. He also told me he didn't want to live and complained about the treatment he was receiving in the hospital. No one spoke to them at all; they just changed their dressings and fed them, nothing else. He had been there thirty days, and his parents could not afford to come visit him.

I went back to my ward and gathered all the guys who could walk to start visiting the amputee wards each day to help the guys who couldn't help themselves with things like eating. Then I saw a wheelchair ramp in one of the hallways, and I got an idea. These guys were bored out of their minds, slowly going crazy, so I thought how much worse could they get hurt? So we got them all out of their beds and took them to the ramp for wheelchair races. We would start them at the top and get them rolling while guys down at the bottom would catch them. They thought it was a hoot and would scream all the way down the ramp, roll onto the floor or be caught by one of the guys, and beg to do it again. We did this for days whenever none of the hospital staff were around.

One doctor found out what we were doing, and he threatened to write us up if we did it again. We knew when he made his rounds, so one day, we stole all of the fire extinguishers and made booby traps with them rigged to a trip wire. When he doctor came through, he tripped the wires and was hit with foam from about six extinguishers at the same time. He was a screaming mess, but he couldn't prove who did it, so the yelling was futile. You don't mess with pissed-off marines.

I remember another eventful night. A black marine I became good friends with asked me to come home with him for the weekend. We stopped at a bar before going to his home in Philadelphia. I was the only white person there. We hadn't even been there ten minutes when someone stabbed another person in the bar. I remember my friend grabbing my arm and saying, "Time to go." We ran from the bar, and he took me to his house. There were about thirty people there of all ages. I walked into the house first, and they were dancing to loud music. As soon as they all saw me standing there, the music stopped, and they started coming at me. My friend stepped in front of me and said, "This is a good friend of mine. He was wounded in Vietnam like me." They all came over and gave me hugs, fed me, gave me drinks, and treated me like I was family. I will never forget that night with a loving family where everyone protected and stood by each other.

I remember when Barb and my son came to visit in her car, we asked him to go to dinner with us. As we approached his neighborhood, he told us to lock all the doors. It wasn't like being at his house. Philadelphia is a place I do not want to return to.

While I was there, they started using Kole and I as military police because they were short on MPs at that time. We were given a weapon and told to take (chase) prisoners from the Philadelphia brig to Quantico, Virginia, where they would be tried and eventually dishonorably discharged. We were given MP uniforms and issued a .45-caliber pistol. We would pick up the prisoners at the Philadelphia brig, and a truck would take us to the railroad station, from which we would ride the train with them to Quantico. When we were given the prisoners, we had to tell them if they ran we would shoot them. We actually had to load our weapons and put a round into the chamber in front of them. They knew we wouldn't shoot them, and we knew we wouldn't shoot them, but it was a game we had to play. Many at the time were being discharged for being discovered to be homosexual or committing minor infractions.

I got sick of running prisoners back and forth and just sitting on the ward. I had Dr. Harris start pushing to get me out of the hospital. She contacted my congressman, and he put pressure on the right people until the orders came through. I had asked the chief several times to get me out of there, and he just ignored me. When the orders came through, they were from Washington. They stated I was to be released from the hospital immediately, after which I would be sent to Cherry Point, North Carolina, to the USMC air base to work in the brig. I spent the rest of my tour working prisoners in the swamps.

EPILOGUE

Barb and Chris moved down to North Carolina with me, and we spent the rest of my tour there. Forty years after I was in Vietnam, I was contacted by the G-2/7 reunion committee. I don't know how they got my name or contact information, but they said they were having a reunion in St. Louis. At that time, I knew Doc McKeen had been killed along with Graham and Corporal Minor, but I didn't know who else had been killed or who would be at the reunion.

I received a call from Cecil and Bob after they also heard about the reunion; it was great talking to them and knowing they had made it back alive. I spoke with them for hours about things I remembered or had forgotten. It reaffirmed what was real and helped separate what I had dreamed after being shot up so bad.

When the reunion came around, I remember seeing Cecil and Bob for the first time since we left Vietnam. We hugged each other and cried on each other's shoulders for a long time. It was like we didn't want to let go. The emotions were unbelievable. I had not expected this, and they hadn't either. Years of bottled-up emotions came out all at once. It was the most humbling experience I have ever had. After crying and hugging for a while, we also met Bobby Donaldson. Bobby was a machine gunner in another platoon, but he was there the day we all got hit. He is a great guy, and he and his wife are now dear friends. We retired to the bar and started telling war stories to each other.

I introduced my son, Chris, to Cecil and Bob, saying, "Remember the helicopter that brought the news of my son the night before we got hit?" They remembered. Again we started crying and hugging. This was our moment in time, and none of us will ever forget. We caught up on everything that had happened in our lives since returning from Vietnam. We discussed our jobs, our wives, our grandchildren, our children, and our time overseas.

My life in the corps is something I will never forget. I will never forget the friends I made, and still have. It is a bond that only marines can understand. I got Barb a set of dog tags and made her an honorary marine after she ran the Marine Corps Marathon. I am very proud of her, and she is my hero. Although the real heroes are the troops from G-2/7 who gave their lives for a war no one wanted to be a part of. No one will ever understand what we did there, why we did it, or why we were there at all.

To those who did not come home, I think of you every day. I know you are with God, and when he met you at the gates, he said, "Good job. Now come and have peace."

Rest in peace, my brothers and friends.

—Jack Morgan
Semper Fidelis